A Tibullus
Reader

BC LATIN Readers

Series Editor:

Ronnie Ancona, Hunter College and CUNY Graduate Center

These readers provide well annotated Latin selections written by experts in the field, to be used as authoritative introductions to Latin authors, genres, topics, or themes for intermediate or advanced college Latin study. Their relatively small size (approximately 600 lines) makes them ideal to use in combination. Each volume includes a comprehensive introduction, bibliography for further reading, Latin text with notes at the back, and complete vocabulary. Nineteen volumes are currently scheduled for publication; others are under consideration. Check our website for updates: www.BOLCHAZY.com.

A Tibullus Reader
Seven Selected Elegies

Paul Allen Miller

Bolchazy-Carducci Publishers, Inc.
Mundelein, Illinois USA

Series Editor: Ronnie Ancona
Volume Editor: Laurie Haight Keenan
Cover Design & Typography: Adam Phillip Velez

A Tibullus Reader
Seven Selected Elegies

Paul Allen Miller

Bolchazy-Carducci Publishers, Inc.
1570 Baskin Road
Mundelein, Illinois 60060
www.bolchazy.com

Printed in the United States of America
2013
by United Graphics

ISBN 978-0-86516-724-7

Library of Congress Cataloging-in-Publication Data

Tibullus.
 [Elegiae. Selections]
 A Tibullus reader : seven selected elegies / Paul Allen Miller.
   pages cm. -- (BC latin readers)
 ISBN 978-0-86516-724-7 (pbk. : alk. paper)
 I. Miller, Paul Allen, 1959- II. Title. III. Series: BC Latin readers.
 PA6787.A3M55 2013
 874'.01--dc23

                                                                    2012041720

Contents

List of Illustrations

Preface

It is hard to think of any more enjoyable way to spend the summer than with the close study of Tibullus. Every time I read him, I am struck again by the subtlety of his verse, the deftness of his humor, and the acuity of his wit. Tibullus is seldom a poet of purple passages and his understated art has frequently gone unnoticed in the modern world. But he was well loved by his Roman readers and it is a great privilege to have this opportunity to bring him to a new generation of Latin students.

I owe a great debt to Ronnie Ancona the series editor for asking me to write this and for her patience as one deadline bled into the next. I also need to thank my wife Ann who has provided patient and unfailing support for my endeavors. Raffaelle Perrelli's invitation to address the conference *Latinum est et legitur* at the University of Calabria in November 2009 on postmodern readings of Tibullus gave me much needed inspiration, and the audience provided valuable feedback. Barbara Gold's commission to write the chapter on Tibullus for the *Blackwell Companion to Latin Elegy* was equally timely and as always her razor sharp pen provided needed correction. Lastly, the Latin students in the spring of 2010 with whom I read pastoral at the University of South Carolina were an unfailing source of inspiration.

The text I have used, while based on Postgate's OCT adopts a number of emendations from other important modern editions. They are noted in the commentary, and the editions are listed in the bibliography. The glossary does not provide complete definitions for the words in question but covers the relevant meanings for the poems. References to passages in the volume and lemmata are in bold. All translations are my own.

I dedicate this volume to the memory of G. Ken Kinman who passed away during the final stages of its composition. He was a soul whose gentle wit and genuine compassion inspired all who knew him. *Ave atque vale!*

Paul Allen Miller
University of South Carolina

Introduction

Tibullus is one of the three canonical Roman elegists and as such is richly deserving of study at all levels. Roman erotic elegy is one of the most influential genres in the history of western poetry. It is not too much to say that our conception of romantic love as the passionate attachment of one person to another was first codified by the Roman elegists. It was from the elegists that the troubadors derived their most famous and influential conceits. Likewise, the love sonnets of the Renaissance poets from Petrarch to Shakespeare would be unimaginable without their elegiac predecessors. The sonnet tradition, in turn, established the conventions for romantic devotion that have dominated western culture ever since. In short, to study the elegiac poets is not just to study a genre of poetry practiced by the far and distant Romans. It is to uncover the storehouse of themes and images from which our modern notions of love and commitment have been constructed.

Of the three major elegists—Tibullus, Propertius, and Ovid—Tibullus is probably today the least appreciated. Yet this was not always the case. Indeed, in antiquity, Tibullus was considered the most accomplished of the three. Quintilian's famous statement, "mihi tersus atque elegans maxime uidetur auctor Tibullus. Sunt qui Propertium malint" ["In my opinion Tibullus is a very elegant and concise author. There are those who prefer Propertius"] (*Inst.* 10.1.93), nicely sums up ancient opinion. Likewise, Ovid terms Tibullus *cultus* or "polished" (*Amores* 3.9.66). The ancients held Tibullus in high regard and valued him above all for his smooth style.

One of the commonplaces of modern Tibullan criticism is a focus on the dream-like quality of his text, a view that normally goes
hand in hand with the devaluation of his poetry as overly soft and
lacking the formal integrity, imaginative leaps, and sharp juxtapositions that characterize Propertius. Others characterize his poetry as
"smooth" and "drifting." It is also widely agreed that Tibullus's poetry is nonlinear and seems to work by association (Veyne 1988: 36).
In the end, his texts are less a series of coherent rhetorical arguments
in the manner of Ovid, than complex tissues of related, interwoven,
and sometimes contradictory themes. The challenge for any intro-
ductory commentary, beyond providing necessary grammatical
help, historical information, and vocabulary glosses is to elucidate
the often difficult and complex nature of these poems.

∾ *The selection*

The elegies selected here are representative of the Tibullan corpus
as a whole. Poems 1.1, 1.5, 2.1, and 2.3 take up the poet's recurring
interest in rural life. They offer a range of views from idealization
in the earlier poems, to a more realist view in poem 2.3. The rural
poems also often associate the country with the mythical Golden
Age, a time of spontaneous natural plenty when men and women
loved openly, and property did not exist. Poems 1.1, 1.2, and 1.5 are
concerned with the poet's first mistress, Delia. Poems 1.4 and 1.9
deal with the topic of homoerotic love and with the poet's pederastic
beloved, Marathus. Poem 2.1 is programmatic for the second book,
reintroducing the poet and his patron, Messalla. Poem 2.3 presents
to us Nemesis, the mistress of the second book. Let us begin by ex-
amining the Delia poems and the presence therein of certain recurrent motifs that define the genre.

Delia poems

Delia herself is clearly a creature of the city, though Tibullus often
dreams of her being with him in the country. Although the exact nature of her identity is never made clear, the most reasonable assumption is that she is a *meretrix* or "courtesan," of the type commonly

found in the comedies of Plautus and Terence. While much of Book 1 is dedicated to Tibullus's love for Delia, the poet also in the same poems dreams of a return to a pastoral, Golden Age, which is deeply at odds with the nature of his erotic desire. The impossibility of squaring this circle is one of the fundamental tensions in the corpus and is well exemplified in all three Delia poems selected for this volume.

We are often reminded in these poems of the shepherds in the *Eclogues*. All is imagined to be ease and contentment. The storms of the world may rage around, but the poet is safe in his rural utopia. Yet, while the Vergialian pastoral world exists largely in a space apart from the cares of the urban life, except for occasional stories about dispossessed shepherds seeking redress and star-crossed lovers, the Tibullan text possesses no such consistency. Tibullus has clearly read his Vergil, but their two universes are not the same. The dreamlike quality that has so often been ascribed to Tibullus's poems consists not only in their escapist elements, but also in their uncanny combination of an idyllic fantasy world with a cold, ironic realism.

The urban world is not only represented by Delia, but also by the poet's patron, Messalla. When the poet is in Rome, however, Tibullus is not pictured as the honored friend of the great man, nor as the quasi-pastoral lover, but either as a humiliated slave chained to the door of his urban mistress or as a locked out lover (*exclusus amator*), who waits before her door while a wealthy rival (*dives amator*) enjoys her favors inside. To a reader familiar with the conventions of elegy, this transition to the poet as slave or object of humiliation may seem less of an affront to common sense than it does to the uninitiated. In the work of all the major elegists, the stance of the poet-lover is often that of the *seruus amoris* or "slave of love." The Delia poems are in some ways the Tibullan poems most typical of the genre.

Homoerotic poems

The Delia poems, while the most frequently anthologized portion of the corpus are not the whole of it. There are also a series of homoerotic poems, poems of a more religious and ceremonial character, and even a new mistress in Book 2, Nemesis. All of these poems, as we shall see, share many of the same themes and stylistic attributes as the more famous Delia poems, but in each case add their own particular variations on them.

In the present collection, we feature two out of the three homoerotic poems from the Tibullan corpus: 1.4 and 1.9. Poem 1.4 presents the phallic god, Priapus, in the guise of another standard elegiac figure, the *praeceptor amoris* ("teacher of love"), while 1.9 revisits this figure as Tibullus tries to assist his beloved, Marathus, in the latter's attempts to win the faithless Pholoe. Homoerotic poems play only a small and largely indirect role in the work of Propertius and virtually no role at all in that of Ovid. But Tibullus's homoerotic poetry may not be as anomalous as the works of the two other surviving canonical elegists would make it seem. We have indications from Propertius (1.20) that homoeroticism may have played a larger role in the work of Cornelius Gallus, than in Ovid and Propertius. Gallus was the first true Roman elegist. Unfortunately, all but a few lines of his work are gone. Nonetheless, in a poem that is universally admitted to be dedicated to Gallus the poet and widely considered derivative of his work, Propertius recounts the tale of Hercules's love for Hylas and the latter's being captured by the nymphs. If this is typical of Gallus's work, then, homoeroticism would have played no small element in it.

Yet we know from a variety of sources that Gallus devoted much of his poetry to his mistress Lycoris. Again the intermixing of heteroerotic and homoerotic poetry may strike a modern audience as odd. But as the last twenty-five years' work on ancient sexuality has amply demonstrated, the concepts of homosexual and heterosexual identity were not operative in the Classical world. Individuals did not define their sexual identities primarily in terms of the gender of their object choice but rather in terms of their active or passive role in the sexual relationship. As with any schema, there were of course exceptions, and the reality of people's erotic lives did not necessarily coincide with the dominant typology that sought to define them. Nonetheless, where we moderns would mark a person who actively pursued both hetero- and homoerotic passions by the term, "bisexual," indicating the unusual combination of two identities normally thought to be distinct, the ancients would have seen no reason to mark such people with a special term, since such behavior would have been considered unremarkable. Thus Catullus, the great predecessor of the elegists, who established many of the forms and themes of elegy but wrote in a wider variety of meters and on a variety of topics, produced in addition to his famous poems about his love for Lesbia a series on Juventius. Likewise, the Alexandrian erotic poetry of Callimachus, the acknowledged inspiration for much of the poetic theory guiding the neoteric and the Augustan poets, was almost exclusively homoerotic in nature.

Book 2

In Tibullus's poetry, then, certain themes recur time and again. Some, like the *praeceptor amoris* ("teacher of love"), the *seruus amoris* ("slave of lover"), and the *diues amator* ("wealthy lover or rival"), are primarily generic and can be found in Propertius and Ovid as well. They are an expected part of the elegiac poet's literary toolbox. Others, however, are more uniquely Tibullan. The focus on the value of rural life, the recollection of the Golden Age, an emphasis on simple piety, and the presence of Messalla are unparalleled in the work of the other elegists or their immediate predecessors, though similar elements can be found in the Vergil of the *Eclogues* and *Georgics*, and perhaps, as Ross and Veyne speculate, in Gallus. These same elements recur in Book 2, where once more they serve as a focus for Tibullus's central concerns but are also rendered IRONIC and ambivalent by their contact with the arch and self-conscious world of elegiac convention.

Poem 2.1 introduces the second book, and it presents us almost exclusively with a world of traditional rural piety. The occasion is the purification rite known as the private Ambarvalia in which a landowner, followed by a procession of dependents—slaves, freedmen, tenant farmers—would lead the sacrifice around the borders of the estate to be purified. Prayer, sacrifice, and general merrymaking would follow the procession. Wine is then brought out and a ritual toast offered to Messalla, a member of the Arval Brothers.

Poem 2.3 returns us to the topic of love in a rural setting. This time, however, Tibullus has a new beloved, Nemesis, and her name is well chosen. In this poem, the dream of the Golden Age has become a nightmare. Nemesis has gone to the country with the poet's wealthy rival, and Tibullus, as the locked-out lover, volunteers to become the literal slave of love, working in the fields of the *diues amator*, if only he can catch a glimpse of his beloved.

∾ Life of the poet

We have very little reliable information about the details of Albius Tibullus's life. He was born between 60 and 55 BCE and is believed to have died in 19. The ancient sources indicate that he came from the Alban Hills east of Rome. As a poet, he dedicates several poems to his patron, Valerius Messalla Corvinus (64 BCE to 8 CE), a famed orator and general, with whom the poet at least once went on campaign. Messalla and his circle supported a group of poets that later included the young Ovid and the lone female elegist, Sulpicia. Messalla, after some initial hesitation, supported Octavian in his conflict with Antony. However, in 27 BCE, he withdrew from political life after celebrating a triumph over the Aquitanians. In poem 2.5, Tibullus celebrates the election (circa 21 BCE) of Messalla's son, Messalinus, to the college of the *quindecimuiri sacris faciundis*, the priests who kept Sibylline oracles. Tibullus is the only one of the three male elegists never to mention Octavian or those in his circle by name. This does not, in fact, mean that Tibullus was unknown to his contemporaries. Horace addresses two poems to him (*Odes* 1.33, *Epistles* 1.4). Ovid writes a moving elegy on his death (*Amores* 3.9). But apart from these too brief testimonia, little is known about the man behind the elegiac persona.

∾ Elegiac meter

Latin and Greek meter is quantitative, that is to say, based on whether a given syllable is long or short. The rules of quantity can be found in any standard grammar. Vowels that are long by nature are marked in the glossary at the back of this book. The elegiac couplet in the hands of the Roman elegists is as much a stylistic as a metrical unit. The first line of each distich is a dactylic hexameter. The second line or pentameter has two parts, consisting of two and a half dactyls apiece:

$$-\underline{\cup\cup}|-\underline{\cup\cup}|-\underline{\cup\cup}|-\underline{\cup\cup}|-\cup\cup|--$$
$$-\underline{\cup\cup}|-\underline{\cup\cup}|-||-\cup\cup|-\cup\cup|-$$

Resolution of the dactyl ($-\cup\cup$) into a spondee ($--$) is common in the hexameter but is rarely found in the fifth foot after Catullus. Resolution is possible in the first half of the pentameter, but not allowed after the caesura or "break" in the line. Elision, or the loss of a syllable ending with a vowel or an *m* at the end of a word positioned in front of a word beginning with vowel or an *h*, is common in the early Latin poets but becomes more restricted in the polished verse of Tibullus and other poets of the Augustan era.

Tibullus's poetry features not only smoothly flowing diction and refined meter but also the frequent use of devices such as internal rhyme (indicated by italics below), to give the couplet a greater aural coherence. Note that each *o* occurs at a metrical break in the couplet:

> Non ego divitias patrum fructusque requir*o*
> quo*s* tulit antiqu*o* || condita messis au*o*. (1.1.41–42)

> [I do not seek the riches and crops of my ancestors,
> what the stored up harvest brought my ancient
> grandfather.]

The resources of the line, here, are exploited for maximum effect. Likewise, the impossibility of spondaic resolution after the pentameter's caesura marks the end of the couplet, sealing it as a complete metrical unit, so that every couplet ends with a metrically identical sequence.

This recurring metrical refrain makes the elegiac couplet less fluid than its cousin, the dactylic hexameter. In Latin after Catullus, each couplet is also a syntactical unit. Elegy is thus not a good meter for extended narrative. But that same structural quality opens up opportunities for rhetorical elaboration. The stanzaic nature of the couplet becomes increasingly marked in later elegiac practice. The emphasis on end-stopped couplets increases over the course of the genre's development so that by the time of Ovid the pentameter invariably finishes with a disyllabic word, doubly marking the closure of the line. This tendency is already clearly visible in Tibullus. As the couplet develops, the hexameter becomes the line of assertion or declaration, while the pentameter becomes that of expansion, qualification, or continuation.

∽ *Suggested readings*

Bright, David F. *Haec Mihi Fingebam: Tibullus in His World*. Leiden: E. J. Brill, 1978.

Cairns, Francis. *Tibullus: A Hellenistic Poet at Rome*. Cambridge: Cambridge University Press, 1979.

Fineberg, Brenda. *Configurations of Desire in the Elegies of Tibullus*. Dissertation. University of Chicago, 1991.

Gildersleeve, B. L., and Gonzalez Lodge. *Gildersleeve's Latin Grammar*. 3rd ed. rev. London: St. Martin's Press, 1895.

James, Sharon. *Learned Girls and Male Persuasion: Gender and Reading in Roman Love Elegy*. Berkeley: University of California Press, 2003.

Kennedy, Duncan. *The Arts of Love: Five Essays in the Discourse of Roman Love Elegy*. Cambridge: Cambridge University Press, 1993.

Lee-Stecum, Parshia. *Powerplay in Tibullus: Reading* Elegies *Book One*. Cambridge: Cambridge University Press, 1998.

Lenz, Fridericus Waltharius, and Godehardus Carolus Galinsky. *Albius Tibullus: Aliorumque Carmina Tres Libri*. Leiden: Brill, 1971.

Luck, Georg. *Tibullus*. Stuttgart: Teubner, 1988.

Maltby, Robert. *Tibullus: Elegies. Text, Introduction, and Commentary*. Cambridge: Francis Cairns, 2002.

Miller, Paul Allen. *Latin Erotic Elegy: An Anthology and Reader.* Routledge: London, 2002.

———. *Subjecting Verses: Latin Love Elegy and the Emergence of the Real.* Princeton: Princeton University Press, 2004.

Murgatroyd, Paul. *Tibullus 1.* Bristol: Bristol Classical Press, 1991 (original Natal, 1980).

———. *Tibullus:* Elegies *II.* Oxford: Oxford University Press, 1994.

Nagy, Gregory. *Comparative Studies in Greek and Indic Meter.* Cambridge, MA: Harvard University Press, 1974.

Perrelli, Raffaele. *Commento a Tibullo:* Elegie, *Libro I.* Soveria Mannelli: Rubbettino, 2002.

Ponchont, Max, ed. *Tibulle et les auteurs du corpus tibullianum.* Paris: Société d'édition, Les Belles-Lettres, 1967.

Putnam, Michael C. J. *Tibullus: A Commentary.* Norman: University of Oklahoma Press, 1973.

Ross, David O., Jr. *Backgrounds to Augustan Poetry: Gallus, Elegy and Rome.* Cambridge, MA: Harvard University Press, 1975.

Smith, Kirby Flower. *The Elegies of Albius Tibullus.* Darmstadt: Wissenschaftliche Buchgesellschaft, 1964 (original 1913).

Veyne, Paul. *Roman Erotic Elegy: Love Poetry and the West.* Translated by David Pellauer. Chicago: University of Chicago Press, 1988.

Latin Text

∾ *Tibullus Book 1*

1.1

Diuitias alius fuluo sibi congerat auro
    et teneat culti iugera multa soli,
quem labor adsiduus uicino terreat hoste,
    Martia cui somnos classica pulsa fugent:
5   me mea paupertas uita traducat inerti,
    dum meus adsiduo luceat igne focus.
ipse seram teneras maturo tempore uites
    rusticus et facili grandia poma manu:
nec Spes destituat sed frugum semper aceruos
10   praebeat et pleno pinguia musta lacu.
nam ueneror, seu stipes habet desertus in agris
    seu uetus in triuio florida serta lapis:
et quodcumque mihi pomum nouus educat annus,
    libatum agricolae ponitur ante deo.
15   flaua Ceres, tibi sit nostro de rure corona
    spicea, quae templi pendeat ante fores;
pomosisque ruber custos ponatur in hortis
    terreat ut saeua falce Priapus aues.

uos quoque, felicis quondam, nunc pauperis agri
20   custodes, fertis munera uestra, Lares.
tunc uitula innumeros lustrabat caesa iuuencos:
        nunc agna exigui est hostia parua soli.
agna cadet uobis, quam circum rustica pubes
        clamet 'io messes et bona uina date.'
25   iam mihi, iam possim contentus uiuere paruo
        nec semper longae deditus esse uiae,
sed Canis aestiuos ortus uitare sub umbra
        arboris ad riuos praetereuntis aquae.
nec tamen interdum pudeat tenuisse bidentem
30   aut stimulo tardos increpuisse boues;
non agnamue sinu pigeat fetumue capellae
        desertum oblita matre referre domum.
at uos exiguo pecori, furesque lupique,
        parcite: de magno praeda petenda grege.
35   hic ego pastoremque meum lustrare quotannis
        et placidam soleo spargere lacte Palem.
adsitis, diui, neu uos e paupere mensa
        dona nec e puris spernite fictilibus.—
fictilia antiquus primum sibi fecit agrestis
40   pocula, de facili composuitque luto.—
non ego diuitias patrum fructusque requiro,
        quos tulit antiquo condita messis auo:
parua seges satis est; satis est, requiescere lecto
        si licet et solito membra leuare toro.
45   quam iuuat immites uentos audire cubantem
        et dominam tenero continuisse sinu

aut, gelidas hibernus aquas cum fuderit Auster,
   securum somnos imbre iuuante sequi!
hoc mihi contingat. sit diues iure, furorem
50   qui maris et tristes ferre potest pluuias.
o quantum est auri pereat potiusque smaragdi,
   quam fleat ob nostras ulla puella uias.
te bellare decet terra, Messalla, marique,
   ut domus hostiles praeferat exuuias:
55   me retinent uinctum formosae uincla puellae,
   et sedeo duras ianitor ante fores.
non ego laudari curo, mea Delia: tecum
   dum modo sim, quaeso segnis inersque uocer.
te spectem, suprema mihi cum uenerit hora,
60   et teneam moriens deficiente manu.
flebis et arsuro positum me, Delia, lecto,
   tristibus et lacrimis oscula mixta dabis.
flebis: non tua sunt duro praecordia ferro
   uincta, nec in tenero stat tibi corde silex.
65   illo non iuuenis poterit de funere quisquam
   lumina, non uirgo sicca referre domum.
tu manes ne laede meos, sed parce solutis
   crinibus et teneris, Delia, parce genis.
interea, dum fata sinunt, iungamus amores:
70   iam ueniet tenebris Mors adoperta caput;
iam subrepet iners aetas, nec amare decebit,
   dicere nec cano blanditias capite.
nunc leuis est tractanda uenus, dum frangere postes
   non pudet et rixas inseruisse iuuat.

75   hic ego dux milesque bonus: uos, signa tubaeque,
             ite procul, cupidis uulnera ferte uiris,
         ferte et opes: ego composito securus aceruo
             dites despiciam despiciamque famem.

1.2

         Adde merum uinoque nouos compesce dolores,
             occupet ut fessi lumina uicta sopor:
         neu quisquam multo percussum tempora baccho
             excitet, infelix dum requiescit amor.
5   nam posita est nostrae custodia saeua puellae,
             clauditur et dura ianua firma sera.
         ianua difficilis domini, te uerberet imber,
             te Iouis imperio fulmina missa petant.
         ianua, iam pateas uni mihi uicta querellis,
10   neu furtim uerso cardine aperta sones.
         et mala si qua tibi dixit dementia nostra,
             ignoscas: capiti sint precor illa meo.
         te meminisse decet quae plurima uoce peregi
             supplice cum posti florida serta darem.
15   tu quoque ne timide custodes, Delia, falle.
             audendum est: fortes adiuuat ipsa Venus.
         illa fauet seu quis iuuenis noua limina temptat
             seu reserat fixo dente puella fores:
         illa docet molli furtim derepere lecto,
20   illa pedem nullo ponere posse sono,
         illa uiro coram nutus conferre loquaces
             blandaque compositis abdere uerba notis.

nec docet hoc omnes, sed quos nec inertia tardat
    nec uetat obscura surgere nocte timor.
25 en ego cum tenebris tota uagor anxius urbe,

      .   .   .   .   .   .

nec sinit occurrat quisquam qui corpora ferro
    uulneret aut rapta praemia ueste petat.
quisquis amore tenetur, eat tutusque sacerque
30   qualibet; insidias non timuisse decet.
non mihi pigra nocent hibernae frigora noctis,
    non mihi cum multa decidit imber aqua.
non labor hic laedit, reseret modo Delia postes
    et uocet ad digiti me taciturna sonum.
35 parcite luminibus, seu uir seu femina fiat
    obuia: celari uult sua furta Venus.
neu strepitu terrete pedum neu quaerite nomen
    neu prope fulgenti lumina ferte face.
si quis et imprudens aspexerit, occulat ille
40   perque deos omnes se meminisse neget:
nam fuerit quicumque loquax, is sanguine natam,
    is Venerem e rapido sentiet esse mari.
nec tamen huic credet coniunx tuus, ut mihi uerax
    pollicita est magico saga ministerio.
45 hanc ego de caelo ducentem sidera uidi,
    fluminis haec rapidi carmine uertit iter,
haec cantu finditque solum manesque sepulcris
    elicit et tepido deuocat ossa rogo:
iam tenet infernas magico stridore cateruas,
50   iam iubet aspersas lacte referre pedem.

cum libet, haec tristi depellit nubila caelo:

    cum libet, aestiuo conuocat orbe niues.

sola tenere malas Medeae dicitur herbas,

    sola feros Hecatae perdomuisse canes.

55   haec mihi composuit cantus, quis fallere posses:

    ter cane, ter dictis despue carminibus.

ille nihil poterit de nobis credere cuiquam,

    non sibi, si in molli uiderit ipse toro.

tu tamen abstineas aliis: nam cetera cernet

60   omnia: de me uno sentiet ille nihil.

quid credam ? nempe haec eadem se dixit amores

    cantibus aut herbis soluere posse meos,

et me lustrauit taedis, et nocte serena

    concidit ad magicos hostia pulla deos.

65   non ego totus abesset amor, sed mutuus esset,

    orabam, nec te posse carere uelim.

ferreus ille fuit qui, te cum posset habere,

    maluerit praedas stultus et arma sequi.

ille licet Cilicum uictas agat ante cateruas,

70   ponat et in capto Martia castra solo,

totus et argento contextus, totus et auro,

    insideat celeri conspiciendus equo;

ipse boues mea si tecum modo Delia possim

    iungere et in solito pascere monte pecus,

75   et te dum liceat teneris retinere lacertis,

    mollis et inculta sit mihi somnus humo.

quid Tyrio recubare toro sine amore secundo

    prodest cum fletu nox uigilanda uenit?

nam neque tunc plumae nec stragula picta soporem

80   nec sonitus placidae ducere posset aquae.

num Veneris magnae uiolaui numina uerbo,

     et mea nunc poenas impia lingua luit?

num feror incestus sedes adiisse deorum

     sertaque de sanctis deripuisse focis?

85   non ego, si merui, dubitem procumbere templis

     et dare sacratis oscula liminibus,

non ego tellurem genibus perrepere supplex

     et miserum sancto tundere poste caput.

at tu, qui laetus rides mala nostra, caueto

90   mox tibi: non uni saeuiet usque deus.

uidi ego qui iuuenum miseros lusisset amores

     post Veneris uinclis subdere colla senem

et sibi blanditias tremula componere uoce

     et manibus canas fingere uelle comas:

95   stare nec ante fores puduit caraeue puellae

     ancillam medio detinuisse foro.

hunc puer, hunc iuuenis turba circumterit arta,

     despuit in molles et sibi quisque sinus.

at mihi parce, Venus: semper tibi dedita seruit

100   mens mea: quid messes uris acerba tuas?

1.4

'Sic umbrosa tibi contingant tecta, Priape,

     ne capiti soles, ne noceantque niues:

quae tua formosos cepit sollertia? certe

     non tibi barba nitet, non tibi culta coma est;

5   nudus et hibernae producis frigora brumae,
      nudus et aestiui tempora sicca Canis.'
sic ego: tum Bacchi respondit rustica proles
      armatus curua sic mihi falce deus.
' o fuge te tenerae puerorum credere turbae:
10   nam causam iusti semper amoris habent.
hic placet, angustis quod equum compescit habenis,
      hic placidam niueo pectore pellit aquam;
hic, quia fortis adest audacia, cepit: at illi
      uirgineus teneras stat pudor ante genas.
15   sed ne te capiant, primo si forte negabit,
      taedia; paulatim sub iuga colla dabit.
longa dies homini docuit parere leones,
      longa dies molli saxa peredit aqua;
annus in apricis maturat collibus uuas,
20   annus agit certa lucida signa uice.
nec iurare time: ueneris periuria uenti
      inrita per terras et freta summa ferunt.
gratia magna Ioui: uetuit Pater ipse ualere,
      iurasset cupide quidquid ineptus amor:
25   perque suas impune sinit Dictynna sagittas
      adfirmes, crines perque Minerua suos.
at si tardus eris errabis. transiet aetas
      quam cito! non segnis stat remeatque dies.
quam cito purpureos deperdit terra colores,
30   quam cito formosas populus alta comas.
quam iacet, infirmae uenere ubi fata senectae,
      qui prior Eleo est carcere missus equus.

uidi iam iuuenem, premeret cum serior aetas,
    maerentem stultos praeteriisse dies.
35   crudeles diui! serpens nouus exuit annos:
    formae non ullam fata dedere moram.
solis aeterna est Baccho Phoeboque iuuentas:
    nam decet intonsus crinis utrumque deum.
tu, puero quodcumque tuo temptare libebit,
40   cedas: obsequio plurima uincet amor.
neu comes ire neges, quamuis uia longa paretur
    et Canis arenti torreat arua siti,
quamuis praetexens picta ferrugine caelum
    uenturam admittat imbrifer arcus aquam.
45   uel si caeruleas puppi uolet ire per undas,
    ipse leuem remo per freta pelle ratem.
nec te paeniteat duros subiisse labores
    aut opera insuetas atteruisse manus;
nec, uelit insidiis altas si claudere ualles,
50   dum placeas, umeri retia ferre negent.
si uolet arma, leui temptabis ludere dextra;
    saepe dabis nudum, uincat ut ille, latus.
tunc tibi mitis erit, rapias tunc cara licebit
    oscula: pugnabit, sed tibi rapta dabit.
55   rapta dabit primo, post adferet ipse roganti,
    post etiam collo se implicuisse uelit.
heu male nunc artes miseras haec saecula tractant:
    iam tener adsueuit munera uelle puer.
at tua, qui uenerem docuisti uendere primus,
60   quisquis es, infelix urgeat ossa lapis.

Pieridas, pueri, doctos et amate poetas,
  aurea nec superent munera Pieridas.
carmine purpurea est Nisi coma: carmina ni sint,
  ex umero Pelopis non nituisset ebur.
65   quem referent Musae, uiuet, dum robora tellus,
  dum caelum stellas, dum uehet amnis aquas.
at qui non audit Musas, qui uendit amorem,
  Idaeae currus ille sequatur Opis,
et tercentenas erroribus expleat urbes
70   et secet ad Phrygios uilia membra modos.
blanditiis uult esse locum Venus ipsa: querellis
  supplicibus, miseris fletibus illa fauet.'
haec mihi, quae canerem Titio, deus edidit ore:
  sed Titium coniunx haec meminisse uetat.
75   pareat ille suae: uos me celebrate magistrum,
  quos male habet multa callidus arte puer.
gloria cuique sua est: me, qui spernentur, amantes
  consultent: cunctis ianua nostra patet.
tempus erit, cum me Veneris praecepta ferentem
80   deducat iuuenum sedula turba senem.
eheu quam Marathus lento me torquet amore!
  deficiunt artes, deficiuntque doli.
parce, puer, quaeso, ne turpis fabula fiam,
  cum mea ridebunt uana magisteria.

1.5

Asper eram et bene discidium me ferre loquebar:
　　at mihi nunc longe gloria fortis abest.
namque agor ut per plana citus sola uerbere turben
　　quem celer adsueta uersat ab arte puer.
5　ure ferum et torque, libeat ne dicere quicquam
　　magnificum post haec: horrida uerba doma.
parce tamen, per te furtiui foedera lecti,
　　per Venerem quaeso compositumque caput.
ille ego cum tristi morbo defessa iaceres
10　te dicor uotis eripuisse meis:
ipseque te circum lustraui sulpure puro,
　　carmine cum magico praecinuisset anus;
ipse procuraui ne possent saeua nocere
　　somnia, ter sancta deueneranda mola;
15　ipse ego uelatus filo tunicisque solutis
　　uota nouem Triuiae nocte silente dedi.
omnia persolui: fruitur nunc alter amore,
　　et precibus felix utitur ille meis.
at mihi felicem uitam, si salua fuisses,
20　fingebam demens sed renuente deo.
rura colam, frugumque aderit mea Delia custos,
　　area dum messes sole calente teret,
aut mihi seruabit plenis in lintribus uuas
　　pressaque ueloci candida musta pede.
25　consuescet numerare pecus; consuescet amantis
　　garrulus in dominae ludere uerna sinu.

illa deo sciet agricolae pro uitibus uuam,
 pro segete spicas, pro grege ferre dapem.
illa regat cunctos, illi sint omnia curae:
30 at iuuet in tota me nihil esse domo.
huc ueniet Messalla meus, cui dulcia poma
 Delia selectis detrahat arboribus:
et, tantum uenerata uirum, hunc sedula curet,
 huic paret atque epulas ipsa ministra gerat.
35 haec mihi fingebam, quae nunc Eurusque Notusque
 iactat odoratos uota per Armenios.
saepe ego temptaui curas depellere uino:
 at dolor in lacrimas uerterat omne merum.
saepe aliam tenui: sed iam cum gaudia adirem,
40 admonuit dominae deseruitque Venus.
tunc me discedens deuotum femina dixit,
 a pudet, et narrat scire nefanda meam.
non facit hoc uerbis, facie tenerisque lacertis
 deuouet et flauis nostra puella comis.
45 talis ad Haemonium Nereis Pelea quondam
 uecta est frenato caerula pisce Thetis.
haec nocuere mihi. quod adest huic diues amator,
 uenit in exitium callida lena meum.
sanguineas edat illa dapes atque ore cruento
50 tristia cum multo pocula felle bibat:
hanc uolitent animae circum sua fata querentes
 semper, et e tectis strix uiolenta canat:
ipsa fame stimulante furens herbasque sepulcris
 quaerat et a saeuis ossa relicta lupis;

55 currat et inguinibus nudis ululetque per urbes,
        post agat e triuiis aspera turba canum.
    eueniet; dat signa deus: sunt numina amanti,
        saeuit et iniusta lege relicta Venus.
    at tu quam primum sagae praecepta rapacis
60   desere: nam donis uincitur omnis amor.
    pauper erit praesto tibi semper: pauper adibit
        primus et in tenero fixus erit latere:
    pauper in angusto fidus comes agmine turbae
        subicietque manus efficietque uiam:
65 pauper ad occultos furtim deducet amicos
        uinclaque de niueo detrahet ipse pede.
    heu canimus frustra nec uerbis uicta patescit
        ianua sed plena est percutienda manu.
    at tu, qui potior nunc es, mea furta timeto:
70   uersatur celeri Fors leuis orbe rotae.
    non frustra quidam iam nunc in limine perstat
        sedulus ac crebro prospicit ac refugit
    et simulat transire domum, mox deinde recurrit
        solus et ante ipsas exscreat usque fores.
75 nescio quid furtiuus amor parat. utere quaeso,
        dum licet: in liquida nam tibi linter aqua.

1.9

    Quid mihi, si fueras miseros laesurus amores,
        foedera per diuos, clam uiolanda, dabas?
    a miser, et si quis primo periuria celat,
        sera tamen tacitis Poena uenit pedibus.

5   parcite, caelestes: aequum est impune licere
         numina formosis laedere uestra semel.
     lucra petens habili tauros adiungit aratro
         et durum terrae rusticus urget opus,
     lucra petituras freta per parentia uentis
10   ducunt instabiles sidera certa rates:
     muneribus meus est captus puer, at deus illa
         in cinerem et liquidas munera uertat aquas.
     iam mihi persoluet poenas, puluisque decorem
         detrahet et uentis horrida facta coma;
15   uretur facies, urentur sole capilli,
         deteret inualidos et uia longa pedes.
     admonui quotiens 'auro ne pollue formam:
         saepe solent auro multa subesse mala.
     diuitiis captus si quis uiolauit amorem,
20   asperaque est illi difficilisque Venus.
     ure meum potius flamma caput et pete ferro
         corpus et intorto uerbere terga seca.
     nec tibi celandi spes sit peccare paranti:
         est deus, occultos qui uetat esse dolos.
25   ipse deus tacito permisit lene ministro,
         ederet ut multo libera uerba mero;
     ipse deus somno domitos emittere uocem
         iussit et inuitos facta tegenda loqui.'
     haec ego dicebam: nunc me fleuisse loquentem,
30   nunc pudet ad teneros procubuisse pedes.
     tunc mihi iurabas nullo te diuitis auri
         pondere, non gemmis, uendere uelle fidem,

non tibi si pretium Campania terra daretur,

   non tibi si, Bacchi cura, Falernus ager.

35   illis eriperes uerbis mihi sidera caeli

   lucere et puras fluminis esse uias.

quin etiam flebas: at non ego fallere doctus

   tergebam umentes credulus usque genas.

quid faciam, nisi et ipse fores in amore puellae?

40   sit, precor, exemplo sit leuis illa tuo.

o quotiens, uerbis ne quisquam conscius esset,

   ipse comes multa lumina nocte tuli!

saepe insperanti uenit tibi munere nostro

   et latuit clausas post adoperta fores.

45   tum miser interii, stulte confisus amari:

   nam poteram ad laqueos cautior esse tuos.

quin etiam attonita laudes tibi mente canebam,

   et me nunc nostri Pieridumque pudet.

illa uelim rapida Vulcanus carmina flamma

50   torreat et liquida deleat amnis aqua.

tu procul hinc absis, cui formam uendere cura est

   et pretium plena grande referre manu.

at te, qui puerum donis corrumpere es ausus,

   rideat adsiduis uxor inulta dolis,

55   et cum furtiuo iuuenem lassauerit usu,

   tecum interposita languida ueste cubet.

semper sint externa tuo uestigia lecto,

   et pateat cupidis semper aperta domus;

nec lasciua soror dicatur plura bibisse

60   pocula uel plures emeruisse uiros.

illam saepe ferunt conuiuia ducere baccho,
  dum rota Luciferi prouocet orta diem.
illa nulla queat melius consumere noctem
  aut operum uarias disposuisse uices.
65 at tua perdidicit, nec tu, stultissime, sentis,
  cum tibi non solita corpus ab arte mouet.
tune putas illam pro te disponere crines
  aut tenues denso pectere dente comas?
ista haec persuadet facies, auroque lacertos
70 uinciat et Tyrio prodeat apta sinu?
non tibi, sed iuueni cuidam uolt bella uideri,
  deuoueat pro quo remque domumque tuam.
nec facit hoc uitio, sed corpora foeda podagra
  et senis amplexus culta puella fugit.
75 huic tamen adcubuit noster puer: hunc ego credam
  cum trucibus uenerem iungere posse feris.
blanditiasne meas aliis tu uendere es ausus?
  tune aliis demens oscula ferre mea?
tum flebis, cum me uinctum puer alter habebit
80 et geret in regno regna superba tuo.
at tua tum me poena iuuet, Venerique merenti
  fixa notet casus aurea palma meos:
'Hanc tibi fallaci resolutus amore Tibullus
  dedicat et grata sis, dea, mente rogat'

❧ *Tibullus Book 2*

2.1

Quisquis adest, faueat: fruges lustramus et agros,
    ritus ut a prisco traditus extat auo.
Bacche, ueni, dulcisque tuis e cornibus uua
    pendeat, et spicis tempora cinge, Ceres.
5 luce sacra requiescat humus, requiescat arator,
    et graue suspenso uomere cesset opus.
soluite uincla iugis: nunc ad praesepia debent
    plena coronato stare boues capite.
omnia sint operata deo: non audeat ulla
10 lanificam pensis imposuisse manum.
uos quoque abesse procul iubeo, discedat ab aris,
    cui tulit hesterna gaudia nocte Venus.
casta placent superis: pura cum ueste uenite
    et manibus puris sumite fontis aquam.
15 cernite, fulgentes ut eat sacer agnus ad aras
    uinctaque post olea candida turba comas.
di patrii, purgamus agros, purgamus agrestes:
    uos mala de nostris pellite limitibus,
neu seges eludat messem fallacibus herbis,
20 neu timeat celeres tardior agna lupos.
tunc nitidus plenis confisus rusticus agris
    ingeret ardenti grandia ligna foco,
turbaque uernarum, saturi bona signa coloni,
    ludet et ex uirgis extruet ante casas.
25 euentura precor: uiden ut felicibus extis
    significet placidos nuntia fibra deos?

nunc mihi fumosos ueteris proferte Falernos
    consulis et Chio soluite uincla cado.
uina diem celebrent: non festa luce madere
30   est rubor, errantes et male ferre pedes.
sed 'bene Messallam' sua quisque ad pocula dicat,
    nomen et absentis singula uerba sonent.
gentis Aquitanae celeber Messalla triumphis
    et magna intonsis gloria uictor auis,
35 huc ades aspiraque mihi, dum carmine nostro
    redditur agricolis gratia caelitibus.
rura cano rurisque deos. his uita magistris
    desueuit querna pellere glande famem:
illi compositis primum docuere tigillis
40   exiguam uiridi fronde operire domum:
illi etiam tauros primi docuisse feruntur
    seruitium et plaustro supposuisse rotam.
tum uictus abiere feri, tum consita pomus,
    tum bibit inriguas fertilis hortus aquas,
45 aurea tum pressos pedibus dedit uua liquores
    mixtaque securo est sobria lympha mero.
rura ferunt messes, calidi cum sideris aestu
    deponit flauas annua terra comas.
rure leuis uerno flores apis ingerit alueo,
50   compleat ut dulci sedula melle fauos.
agricola adsiduo primum satiatus aratro
    cantauit certo rustica uerba pede
et satur arenti primum est modulatus auena
    carmen, ut ornatos diceret ante deos,

55   agricola et minio suffusus, Bacche, rubenti

        primus inexperta duxit ab arte choros.

huic datus a pleno memorabile munus ouili

        dux pecoris: curtas auxerat hircus opes.

rure puer uerno primum de flore coronam

60   fecit et antiquis imposuit Laribus.

rure etiam teneris curam exhibitura puellis

        molle gerit tergo lucida uellus ouis.

hinc et femineus labor est, hinc pensa colusque,

        fusus et adposito pollice uersat opus:

65   atque aliqua adsidue textrix operata Mineruae

        cantat, et a pulso tela sonat latere.

ipse quoque inter agros interque armenta Cupido

        natus et indomitas dicitur inter equas.

illic indocto primum se exercuit arcu:

70   ei mihi, quam doctas nunc habet ille manus!

nec pecudes, uelut ante, petit: fixisse puellas

        gestit et audaces perdomuisse uiros.

hic iuueni detraxit opes, hic dicere iussit

        limen ad iratae uerba pudenda senem:

75   hoc duce custodes furtim transgressa iacentes

        ad iuuenem tenebris sola puella uenit

et pedibus praetemptat iter suspensa timore,

        explorat caecas cui manus ante uias.

a miseri, quos hic grauiter deus urget! at ille

80   felix, cui placidus leniter adflat Amor.

sancte, ueni dapibus festis, sed pone sagittas

        et procul ardentes hinc precor abde faces.

uos celebrem cantate deum pecorique uocate
    uoce: palam pecori, clam sibi quisque uocet.
85   aut etiam sibi quisque palam: nam turba iocosa
    obstrepit et Phrygio tibia curua sono.
ludite: iam Nox iungit equos, currumque sequuntur
    matris lasciuo sidera fulua choro,
postque uenit tacitus furuis circumdatus alis
90   Somnus et incerto Somnia nigra pede.

2.3

Rura meam, Cornute, tenent uillaeque puellam:
    ferreus est, heu heu, quisquis in urbe manet.
ipsa Venus latos iam nunc migrauit in agros,
    uerbaque aratoris rustica discit Amor.
5   o ego, cum aspicerem dominam, quam fortiter illic
    uersarem ualido pingue bidente solum
agricolaeque modo curuum sectarer aratrum,
    dum subigunt steriles arua serenda boues!
nec quererer quod sol graciles exureret artus,
10   laederet et teneras pussula rupta manus.
pauit et Admeti tauros formosus Apollo,
    nec cithara intonsae profueruntue comae,
nec potuit curas sanare salubribus herbis:
14   quidquid erat medicae uicerat artis amor.
14a   ipse deus solitus stabulis expellere uaccas

14b   et miscere nouo docuisse coagula lacte,
14c   lacteus et mixtus obriguisse liquor.

15   tunc fiscella leui detexta est uimine iunci,
         raraque per nexus est uia facta sero.
      o quotiens illo uitulum gestante per agros
         dicitur occurrens erubuisse soror!
      o quotiens ausae, caneret dum ualle sub alta,
20   rumpere mugitu carmina docta boues!
      saepe duces trepidis petiere oracula rebus,
         uenit et a templis inrita turba domum:
      saepe horrere sacros doluit Latona capillos,
         quos admirata est ipsa nouerca prius.
25   quisquis inornatumque caput crinesque solutos
         aspiceret, Phoebi quaereret ille comam.
      Delos ubi nunc, Phoebe, tua est, ubi Delphica Pytho?
         nempe Amor in parua te iubet esse casa.
      felices olim, Veneri cum fertur aperte
30   seruire aeternos non puduisse deos.
      fabula nunc ille est: sed cui sua cura puella est,
         fabula sit mauult quam sine amore deus.
      at tu, quisquis is es, cui tristi fronte Cupido
         imperat ut nostra sint tua castra domo

35   ferrea non uenerem sed praedam saecula laudant:
         praeda tamen multis est operata malis.
      praeda feras acies cinxit discordibus armis:
         hinc cruor, hinc caedes mors propiorque uenit.
      praeda uago iussit geminare pericula ponto,
40   bellica cum dubiis rostra dedit ratibus.

praedator cupit immensos obsidere campos,
 ut multa innumera iugera pascat oue:
cui lapis externus curae est, urbisque tumultu
 portatur ualidis mille columna iugis,
45 claudit et indomitum moles mare, lentus ut intra
 neglegat hibernas piscis adesse minas.
at mihi laeta trahant Samiae conuiuia testae
 fictaque Cumana lubrica terra rota.
heu heu diuitibus uideo gaudere puellas:
50 iam ueniant praedae, si Venus optat opes
ut mea luxuria Nemesis fluat utque per urbem
 incedat donis conspicienda meis.
illa gerat uestes tenues, quas femina Coa
 texuit, auratas disposuitque uias:
55 illi sint comites fusci, quos India torret
 Solis et admotis inficit ignis equis:
illi selectos certent praebere colores
 Africa puniceum purpureumque Tyros.
nota loquor: regnum ipse tenet, quem saepe coegit
60 barbara gypsatos ferre catasta pedes.
at tibi, dura seges, Nemesim qui abducis ab urbe,
 persoluat nulla semina certa fide.
et tu, Bacche tener, iucundae consitor uuae,
 tu quoque deuotos, Bacche, relinque lacus.
65 haud impune licet formosas tristibus agris
 abdere: non tanti sunt tua musta, pater.
o ualeant fruges, ne sint modo rure puellae:
 glans alat et prisco more bibantur aquae.

glans aluit ueteres, et passim semper amarunt:
70   quid nocuit sulcos non habuisse satos?
tunc, quibus aspirabat Amor, praebebat aperte
    mitis in umbrosa gaudia ualle Venus.
nullus erat custos, nulla exclusura dolentes
75   ianua: si fas est, mos precor ille redi.

horrida uillosa corpora ueste tegant.
nunc si clausa mea est, si copia rara uidendi,
    heu miserum, laxam quid iuuat esse togam ?
ducite: ad imperium dominae sulcabimus agros:
80   non ego me uinclis uerberibusque nego.

Commentary

ꙮ *1.1*

Tibullus's poems are sometimes compared to symphonic compositions. They are less linear arguments than elaborate arrangements of and variations on repeated themes. In this first poem, we have an initial fantasy of rural ease (**1–43**), which brings to mind various recollections of the Golden Age found in pastoral poetry and elsewhere in Tibullus, followed by a brief transitional passage in which the amatory theme is first introduced (**43–52**). The poem closes with a brief evocation of the poet's patron Messalla, and then the focus shifts from the country to the city and from the joys to the trials of love (**53–76**), before returning in a brief coda to the initial theme of satisfaction with a modest sufficiency (**77–78**).

The transitions between these sections are often subtle. At the same time, recurring motifs found throughout the poem, often embodied in repeated words (*facilis, iners, paruus, pudet*), thematic oppositions (wealth versus poverty), and character types (the soldier, the merchant, and the slave) give the poem a larger coherence. "What poses as artless nonchalance is in fact a carefully crafted interweaving of ideas and poetic language" (Miller 2002: 121).

Poem 1.1 begins in the subjunctive mood. It does not indicate a state of affairs, but rather a set of desires. These desires are nothing unusual in the poetry of the period: wishes for a return to country piety, for ease, and for love. Yet, while the desires are familiar, they do not in Tibullus 1.1 seem to emanate from any one, easily recognizable speaker. Who is this man expressing these wishes: a farmer, a soldier, a dissolute lover? All have been posited. Where is he located in physical, ideological, or social space? None of these things is made clear, and initial answers often seem to be contradicted by

later developments as the reader moves through the poem. Tibullan poetics, as they are announced in the opening poem of his first
collection, are more about suggestions than statements, more about
desires than reality, more about questions than answers.

Delia herself is clearly a creature of the city, though Tibullus often
dreams of her being with him in the country. In point of fact, while
much of Book 1 is dedicated to his love for Delia, the poet's dream
of a return to a pre-urban, Golden Age is deeply at odds with the nature of his erotic desire. This contradiction is one of the fundamental
tensions animating the corpus and is well exemplified in this poem.
Thus, midway through, the poet writes:

> parua seges satis est; satis est, requiescere lecto
>   si licet et solito membra leuare toro.
> quam iuuat immites uentos audire cubantem   45
>   et dominam tenero continuisse sinu.

> [A little field is enough. It is enough if it is permitted
> to rest in bed and to put up your feet on your
> accustomed couch. How it makes you happy to lie
> down and to hear the bitter winds and to hold your
> mistress on your tender breast!] (1.1.43–46).

In this passage, we find a vision typical of the Tibullan rural idyll.
The humble farmer enjoys his peaceful rest. We are reminded of the
shepherds in the *Eclogues* resting from the summer heat in the shade
of a nearby cave as a brook babbles by. All is ease and contentment
after honest labor. The storms of the world may rage around—greed,
politics, the civil wars that had wracked Rome for the past hundred
years—but the poet is safe in his pastoral world with his mistress nes-
tled against him.

Yet, while this pastoral world exists largely in a space apart from
the cares of the urban life, except for occasional stories about dispossessed shepherds seeking redress and star-crossed lovers, the Tibullan text possesses no such consistency of world. Tibullus has clearly
read his Vergil, but their two fictive universes are not the same. The

dreamlike quality that has so often been ascribed to Tibullus's poems consists not only in their escapist elements, but also in the uncanny combination of an idyllic fantasy world with a cold, IRONIC realism, sometimes even satire. Thus less than ten lines after this initial passage, we are yanked from the dream of pastoral ease and thrown into a world of power, politics, and personal humiliation:

> te bellare decet terra, Messalla, marique,
>   ut domus hostiles praeferat exuuias:
> me retinent uinctum formosae uincla puellae,   55
>   et sedeo duras ianitor ante fores.

> [It is fitting, Messalla, that you wage wars on land and
> sea so that your house may display enemy spoils: the
> chains of a beautiful girl hold me bound and I sit a
> door-keeper before her hard doors]. (1.1.53–56)

In these lines, there is an almost cinematic cut from the fantasy world of rural ease examined earlier to the entrance to the house of the poet's patron, M. Valerius Messalla Corvinus. The presence of the latter introduces another recurring motif in the corpus, represented in this selection of poems by the current passage, an important appearance in 1.5, and a central role in 2.1. Messalla represents the normative social world of Rome. He defines *uirtus* (manliness, courage, virtue) and *gloria* (honor, glory). After initially siding with Antony in the conflict with Octavian that broke out when the assassins of Julius Caesar were defeated at Philippi (42 BCE), Messalla switched sides and went on, later, in 31 BCE, to serve as consul with the future Augustus in the same year he would defeat Antony at Actium. Messalla was later governor of Gaul from 28–27 BCE, during which time he conquered the Aquitani. In 27 BCE, he was the last person outside the imperial family to celebrate a triumph. He was also a distinguished patron of poets. In addition to Tibullus, he would later have Ovid in his circle as well as his niece Sulpicia, the lone female Roman elegist. According to the ancient life of the poet, Tibullus served under Messalla in the Aquitanian campaign and was in fact no stranger to the military life he affects to reject. Messalla, then, the descendant of an important aristocratic family, represents the image of Roman respectability: military conquest, political success, and cultural achievement.

The shift to Messalla and the glory of his house is a shift from the world of the rural idyll to that of contemporary, urban Rome. In the very next couplet, we pan to a very different house. There, Tibullus sits, not as the honored friend of the great man, nor as the quasi-pastoral lover, but as a humiliated slave chained to the door of his urban mistress. In the latter third of 1.1, we move quickly from the poet's fantasy of rural ease and erotic fulfillment, to the glittering aristocratic house of Messalla with its displays of captured booty (*exuuiae*), to the door of Delia's house in the city.

For a reader familiar with the conventions of the elegiac genre, this transition to the poet as slave may seem less of an affront to common sense than it does to the newcomer. In the work of all the major elegists, one common stance of the poet-lover is that of the *seruus amoris* or "slave of love." This is a figure that has deep roots in Greek erotic poetry, where it figures almost exclusively in a pederastic context. What the Roman elegists add that is fundamentally new, beginning with their great precursor Catullus, is the figure of the "mistress" or *domina*. Hence, one of the trademark features of Roman erotic elegy is the subjection of a Roman aristocratic man— all the major elegists were members of the wealthy and increasingly powerful equestrian order, just beneath the senatorial order—to a woman. This is a situation that in real life would have been considered an irrecoverable humiliation. In the elegiac context, however, it is completely expected. Moreover, in all the elegists after Catullus, the *domina* is commonly portrayed as a *meretrix* or "courtesan," that is to say as a freedwoman who provided sophisticated companionship and sexual services in return for economic support. Thus the figure of *seruus amoris* in elegy represents a double humiliation: a Roman man of the aristocratic strata seemingly subjects himself to a female member of the lower orders. That humiliation is compounded in this scene where Tibullus portrays himself as a *ianitor*, one of the lowest members of the servile order, a slave who was chained to the door of his master or mistress. Roman elegy asks us to laugh at such a spectacle of subjection, even as it creates an IRONIC double perspective that also invites us to identify with the poet and his passion. If we do not recognize the pathos of the situation, the humor quickly becomes shallow and one-dimensional. If we do not see the humor, then the rapid juxtapositions become signs of failure if not incoherence. The Tibullan text is, in fact, a highly sophisticated verbal artifact and far from a simple confession or description of the poet's erotic life.

To the connoisseur of elegiac poetry, the appearance of the motif of *seruitium amoris*, then, would not in itself have been surprising and might well have been expected. Nonetheless, its rapid appearance has a disorienting effect. If the life of conquest and glory is fitting for Messalla, why is it not for the poet? Should his humiliation be seen as real or something he in fact glories in? Are the two doorways, Messalla's and Delia's, in some sense equivalent, each appropriate to its owner or to the slave that sits before them? But what does that say about the nature of Messalla's glory if in fact it can in any way be said to be equivalent to that of a *meretrix* or her slave? There is something comical about this juxtaposition. But it can be very difficult to say precisely who or what the butt of the joke is. Moreover, if in fact, Tibullus is a slave chained to the door of Delia in the city, what are we to make of the elaborate rural fantasy, which takes up the first fifty-two lines of the poem? Was it just a pose? Where in fact does the poet's desire really lie?

Or are these the wrong questions? As in a dream, would it be a mistake to assume a single unified intent behind the poem? Might not the desire for pastoral escape, the desire for social recognition and approval represented by Messalla, and the desire for erotic fulfillment and even humiliation all coexist in an uneasy tension, in the same way that competing desires and images coexist within a dream? Moreover, if we reread the whole poem from the perspective of a contemporary Roman citizen, who would know that Tibullus was himself an aristocrat who had been on campaign with Messalla, would not the humor and the IRONY of both his rural dream and his supposed urban subjection be only heightened? Where does the center of gravity for this poem lie?

It is precisely this very intense level of complexity and lack of clear answers that often makes Tibullus a challenge for first-time readers. We want to know what he really meant, which one of these competing voices we are to listen to. Yet, the absolute ease and sophistication of his verse, the smoothness of his transitions, make it equally possible to read these poems and be undisturbed by such questions. Again, like a dream, it is less in the moment of actual dreaming or of reading that we are puzzled by the nature of the text's structure and the contradictory desires it seems to express, than later when we reflect back on our experience and try rationally to explain it. The problem is less in Tibullus's text than in our modern assumption that it should express the unified intent of a person we immediately recognize and with whom we can identify ourselves.

1–4   The first word of a poem often served as its title. Yet, *diuitias*, "riches," are not the object of praise in this poem but rather rural simplicity. Only in the second couplet do we realize that the person in question is a soldier and not a wealthy farmer.

Note that all the main verbs are in the subjunctive, indicating a wished-for state of affairs, rather than a statement of fact.

3–4   **labor** = both "labor" and "struggle," the opposite of the *uita iners* described in **5**

Martia . . . somnos classica pulsa fugent The martial trumpet blast routing sleep stands in contrast to the later image of the poet slumbering with his beloved while a storm rages outside (see **45–46**). Sleep or a dreamlike state is the ideal for the Tibullan lover. *Fugo* is common in military contexts.

5–6   Rome was a plutocracy, and from the perspective of the aristocratic classes to wish for poverty (*paupertas*) would have been perverse. Nonetheless, the small farmer was traditionally considered the backbone of Rome. He was revered for his hard work and dedication to the state. Tibullus plays upon this tradition, while striking the pose of an outsider, of one who rejects the pursuit of wealth and honors characteristic of aristocratic life in Rome.

me mea Note the play on similar words, PARANOMASIA.

traducat is difficult to translate. It should mean "hand over" or "entrust," but it can also mean "expose" or "traduce." Both senses are in play. Tibullus through his fantasy of rural ease has put his finger on a contradiction at the very heart of traditional Roman ideology. The farmer-soldier is split into two antithetical images whose common ground is alluded to in the repetition of *adsiduus*. In line **3**, it modified *labor*; here it modifies the fire (*igne*) in the farmer's hearth (*focus*). Yet, labor is the condition of the farmer as much as it is of the soldier, and in each case the opposite of the *uita iners* for which the poet longs.

luceat = subjunctive after *dum* in a conditional wish. See Gildersleeve and Lodge ¶ 573.

7-8   **rusticus** is an odd adj. for a poet who in neoteric terms should be *urbanus*. These terms are more stylistic than geographic. An *urbanus* is one who speaks and acts in the style of the city, i.e., with wit and sophistication. The *rusticus* is his opposite: a rube, a bumpkin. "*Ipse* emphasizes the strangeness of an equestrian planting and sowing with his own hands. Of course, manual labor as the object of fantasy represents the height of sophistication. It can be a dream only to those for whom it is not a fact of daily life" (Miller 2002: 122).

The pairing of *teneras* with *maturo* alludes to the entire agricultural cycle from planting to the harvest of ripe fruit. *Poma* is SYNECDOCHE for *pomus*, the tree itself. *Ipse seram* in 7 has both *teneras . . .uites* and *grandia poma* as direct objects. The language is very condensed.

facili . . . manu is difficult. *Facilis* should mean "easy, without effort." However, the labor described is hardly effortless. Many argue for a less common, act. meaning, "ready, skillful." But, of course, if the farmer's life is to be contrasted with the soldier's on the basis of who endures more *adsiduus labor*, then the idea of ease, no matter how nonsensical in the real word, cannot be discarded.

9–10   Note the images of abundance even in the context of the *pau-pertas* of line 5.

lacu = "vat"

pinguia musta = "rich new-pressed wine"

11–12   The poet asserts his traditional piety. This couplet features the first verbs in the indicative. The poem as whole represents a dream or wish, and the subjunctive mood predominates.

The worship of stumps (*stipes*) and stones (*lapis*), used as boundary markers often at crossroads (*triuio*), was a common aspect of early Roman religion, which featured a series of animistic cults honored by small farmers.

stipes and *lapis* are each the subject of *habet*.

13–14   First fruits are offered to the god of the farmer, deliberately vague, but possibly Priapus.

Note *ēducō* is not *ēdūcō*.

libatum = supine from *libo*, meaning "for a sacrifice"

15–16   Special offerings are reserved for Ceres as goddess of the grain harvest. We return to the jussive subjunctive.

flaua Ceres = vocative

corona spicea = a crown made of ears of grain, an offering that dates to the very beginnings of Roman religion

17–18   Red (*ruber*) painted statues of the phallic god Priapus were often used as scarecrows in Roman gardens and orchards.

19–20   The former prosperity of a farm is a common theme in pastoral poetry of the period and is generally thought to allude to the proscriptions during the civil war, when land was seized for political purposes and the owners often executed. Compare *Eclogues* 1. Note the reversion to the indicative to discuss fallen reality as opposed to longed-for fantasy.

pauperis *Paupertas* for the Roman elite did not signify abject poverty, but rather the inability to live in manifest wealth.

fertis here has the less common meaning, "accept an offering" (Maltby 2002).

Lares = household gods, charged with protecting the whole of the estate. Vocative in apposition with *custodes*.

21–22　In the past, the farm had numberless cattle. Now the sacrifice of a single lamb can purify the entire herd.

hostia = predicate nom.

soli is gen. with *exigui*.

23–24　The poet imagines a typical rustic ceremony with the local youths gathered round to pray for the harvest and plentiful wine.

cadet The shift to the fut. indicative completes the cycle begun with the impf. in line 21 (*lustrabat*), progressing to the pres. (*est*), and continuing on to the fut. The break with the past is irrecoverable, but the continuity of ritual life endures.

circum = postpositive with *quam*, the antecedent of which is *agna*

clamet = jussive subjunctive

io = an exclamation frequently found in ritual contexts

date = imperative addressed to the *Lares*

25–26　The hortatory *possim* ("may I be able") implies that the dream of a simple life represents in part a struggle to live under reduced circumstances. The agrarian ideal is, on one level, an attempt to make the best of a bad situation. On another, it reveals the IRONIC humor of a sophisticated equestrian in first-century Rome proclaiming such humble dreams. Note the emphatic repetition of *iam*.

paruo = substantive

longae ... uiae In Tibullus long voyages are signs of greed and corruption associated with the end of the Golden Age.

deditus esse = pf. infinitive < *dedo*

27–28　Instead of the voyages of the soldier and merchant, the poet longs to be contented with the pastoral paradise described in Vergil's *Eclogues* and Theocritus's *Idylls*.

Canis The rising of the Dog Star marks the hottest days of summer.

uitare depends on *possim* in **25**.

praetereuntis = gen. sing. pres. pple. < *praetereo*

29-30 The hortatory subjunctive, *pudeat*, indicates that for many it would be a source of shame for a person of Tibullus's status to perform manual labor.

tenuisse and **increpuisse** = pf. infinitives, common in Augustan poetry, especially elegy, in place of the pres. This bit of literary preciosity stands in contrast to the longed-for simplicity.

31-32 The mildly comic pathos of the poet carrying back the lost lamb or kid is not to be missed. Note the return to the pres. infinitive.

oblita matre = abl. absolute. *oblita* < *obliuiscor*.

domum = acc. of limit of motion (Gildersleeve and Lodge ¶ 337),"to the house"

33-34 Thieves and wolves should spare the small herd and rob the rich.

exiguo pecori = dat. complement of *parcite*

petenda assumes *est*: pass. periphrastic.

35-36 The poet as landowner carries out the timeless rituals of the Italian countryside.

pastorem . . . meum = the slave who kept watch over the flocks. Tibullus does not imagine a servile life, as Vergil does in the *Eclogues*, but the life of the modest landowner in opposition to the soldier, merchant, or urban mogul. Compare **2.1**.

Palem = Pales, the goddess of herds and flocks. Her holiday, the Parilia, was celebrated every year on April 21, the foundation day of Rome. The ritual libation consisted of milk (*lacte*) and oil.

37-38 Let the gods not spurn the simple piety of days gone by.

adsitis a return to the jussive subjunctive common in ritual invitations

diui archaic nom. pl. of *deus*

fictilibus = substantive: earthenware, as opposed to gold or silver plate

39-40 The poet flashes back to a simpler time in which the clay yielded easily to the rustic potter's hand.

Note the repetition of *fictilia* and its etymological connection with *fecit* and *facili*. The word *poeta* in Greek means "maker."

fictilia ... pocula = direct object of both *fecit* (39) and *composuit* (40)

agrestis = substantive

facili Again the emphasis is on rural ease. Compare **8**.

41-42 The poet concludes this section of the poem by recapitulating the themes articulated in **19–22**.

diuitias takes us all the way back to **1**. For more on this couplet, see the "Introduction," under "Elegiac Meter."

The antecedent of *quos* = *fructus*.

43-44 The poet here begins to make the transition to his second, major theme. But observe how *parua seges satis est* makes it appear that the agricultural theme will continue. This impression is compounded by the repetition of *satis est*. The subtleness of his transitions is a major component in the dreamlike quality of Tibullan verse. The mention of the bed (*lecto*) and the couch (*toro*) are the first signs that the poet's attention is changing. *Torus* often carries the meaning of "marriage bed."

45-48 **audire, continuisse,** and **sequi** are complements of *iuuat*. Each of these infinitives has an acc. subject (*cubantem* for *audire* and *continuisse*; *securum* for *sequi*).

45-46 The image of the lover listening to the storm, while embracing his mistress, stands in sharp contrast to the lot of the soldier or merchant. With the entrance of the *domina*, the theme of the *seruus amoris* is never far behind. See **55**.

cubantem = substantive, but the referent is indef. On the one hand, the pres. pple. could modify an implied *me*. On the other, it could modify an assumed *quemquem*. The use of the substantive artfully allows the poet to have it both ways.

continuisse = pf. infinitive < *contineo*. See **29–30**.

47-48   The previous theme continues.

Auster The south wind over the Mediterranean brings clouds and rain in the winter.

securum . . . sequi is structurally parallel to *audire . . . cubantem.*

somnos . . . sequi a direct contrast with the life of the soldier as depicted in **4**. The phrase is striking.

iuuante recalls *iuuat* in **45**.

49-50   The switch back to the jussive subjunctive (*contingat*) indicates that the state of affairs in **45–48**, although described in the indicative, is merely longed for.

sit diues iure It should be the case that only the rich man can (and therefore does) bear the fury of the sea. *iure* = "by right, rightly"

furorem = direct object of *ferre* along with *pluuias*. There is a mild HYPERBATON or disturbance of normal word order.

Note that this is the first of three rhyming couplets (*pluuias . . . uias . . . exuuias*), drawing the rural portion of the poem to a close before introducing Messalla in **54**.

51-52   Better that gold and riches perish from the earth than my girl shed a tear.

quantum est + partitive gen. = "however much there is of x," a colloquial expression not found elsewhere in Tibullus or the elegists

potiusque . . . quam = "rather than." Logically the *-que* should go at the end of *smaragdi*.

smaragdi This Greek word for a precious stone, despite the double consonant at its beginning, does not make position for the preceding short vowel.

uias Compare **26**.

53-54   For the poet's patron, Mesalla, the life of battle on land and seas is proper. Is this a recognition of different callings being appropriate to different stations, an undercutting of Messalla's preeminence, or an acknowledgment of the abject position of the Tibullan lover vis-à-vis the norms of Roman aristocratic behavior? The text allows for all three readings, and its IRONIC indeterminacy is central to Tibullan poetics.

55-56 The *ianitor* was among the most menial of servile positions. Chained to the door, he guarded access to the house. The poet here combines two common tropes of love elegy: the *seruus amoris* and the *exclusus amator*. The IRONY is that while it would normally be the function of the *ianitor* to keep the lover locked out, the poet here remains "chained" to the door of his *domina*, but as we see in 1.2, he is chained to the outside. A further level of irony is the contrast between the glory of Messalla's vestibule and the humiliation of the poet.

retinent We are no longer in the world of the subjunctive but the pres. indicative.

57-58 The refusal of praise would strike any member of the honor-obsessed Roman aristocracy as comical at best, perverse at worst.

tecum = *cum te*

dum modo + subjunctive = "so long as." Compare **6.**

iners See **5** and **71.**

uocer = 1ˢᵗ person sing. pres. pass. subjunctive in an indirect command after *quaeso*

59-60 Fantasies of the poet's death are a recurring feature of elegiac poetry and perhaps a remnant of the meter's connection with funereal inscriptions and songs of lament.

te = direct object of *spectem* and *teneam*

suprema = "final," superl. of *superus*

61-62 **arsuro** = fut. act. pple. < *ardeo*, modifying *lecto*. Note that the bed of love in **43** has now become the funeral bier.

Delia the first time she is named

lacrimis oscula mixta the apotheosis of love's bittersweet nature

63–64   Delia's tears at Tibullus's fantasized funeral are the hoped-for proof that she is not hardhearted. Note the ANAPHORIC repetition of *flebis*. ANAPHORA is one of Tibullus's most common stylistic devices. He uses it to create emphasis, to group couplets in to larger compositional units, and to mark transitions. The commentary will point out a number of instances throughout the selection.

65–66   One of the elegist's standard roles is as *praeceptor amoris* to those less experienced. His young pupils will leave his funeral in tears.

domum = acc. of limit of motion (Gildersleeve and Lodge ¶ 337)

67–68   The poet forbids Delia to engage in the familiar ritual signs of mourning—tearing of the hair and cheeks—since it will mar her beauty.

ne with the imperative *laede* = archaic and poetic; *ne* + subjunctive would be the usual construction.

Note the all-but-rhyming line endings: *parce solutis* and *parce genis*.

69–70   The poet skillfully modulates from his lurid death fantasies into the more familiar *carpe diem* motif: "let us love while we can!"

Mors Death is vividly PERSONIFIED with its head shrouded in darkness (*tenebris*). The image is unparalleled in Latin literature.

caput = Greek acc. of respect

71–72   Creeping age will soon render love indecent.

iners Compare **3** and **58**.

decebit recalls *decet* in **53**.

dicere . . . blanditias to speak sweet nothings

73–74   In youth, behavior that would otherwise be considered disgraceful is widely tolerated. This is a truism of Roman comedy.

leuis is the opposite of *grauis*: love is light, trivial, fickle. It does not exhibit the *grauitas* expected of the Roman adult male.

est tractanda = pass. periphrastic

non pudet Contrast with **29**'s *nec pudeat.*

75–76   In the last lines of the first poem, the poet does a veritable catalog of amatory poses: *seruus amoris, exclusus amator, praeceptor amoris*, and here *militia amoris*. The "soldiery of love" is a common parody of the normative Roman emphasis on martial virtues. In evoking it, the poet plays a variation on the themes first announced at the poem's beginning.

ite = imperative < *eo*

cupidis . . . uiris Note the ambiguity. Are these men who "desire" wounds and have therefore become soldiers or "desiring men" like the lover himself? Might they not also be "greedy" men, those afflicted with "cupidity"?

77–78   The poet does not advocate poverty, but satisfaction with what is sufficient. Wealth belongs to those who risk their lives to get it. Compare **49–50**.

aceruo See line **9**.

dites despiciam despiciamque tamem This final line is a tour de force, making use of ALLITERATION, repetition, and CHIASTIC balance to drive home the poet's avowed commitment to the "mean" or a position between wealth and hunger.

∾ *1.2*

Poem 1.2 picks up where 1.1 left off. The poet has not simply re-
corded his feelings, but he has consciously constructed a book. The
previous poem ends with the poet breaking down the beloved's door.
In poem 1.2, the second of our Delia poems, the dream of rural ease
is all but gone, and we find the poet before Delia's door seeking to be
let in. He is in distress. Delia has been placed under guard, and he
has been locked out:

> nam posita est nostrae custodia saeua puellae,   5
>   clauditur et dura ianua firma sera.
> ianua difficilis domini, te uerberet imber,
>   te Iouis imperio fulmina missa petant.
> ianua, iam pateas uni mihi uicta querellis,
>   neu furtim uerso cardine aperta sones. (1.2.5–10)

A reader familiar with the conventions of the elegiac genre will find
much that she or he will recognize. The poet finds himself in the
position of the *exclusus amator* or "locked out" lover. What follows
normally is a poetic performance designed to persuade the door, the
beloved, the *ianitor*, or all three to let the poet in. That performance
is known as a *paraclausithyron*.

The fact that Delia is held by a *dominus* or "master," moreover, indicates that she does not wholly possess her freedom. There is no reason to suppose she is servile per se, but the fact that she has a master,
who clearly feels he has proprietary rights over how she disposes of
her own body, indicates that she is no freeborn daughter of a Roman
aristocrat or of a respectable *matrona*. The *dominus* would most likely
be a lover who has paid, either through gifts, money, or material support, for her services and therefore feels entitled to an exclusive claim
on them. Delia, like most other elegiac mistresses, would be a freedwoman who is the dependent of her *dominus* (see James, 2002).

One of the implications of this scenario is that elegiac love, while
not necessarily adulterous, is never legitimate. The *domina* is under the rule (*manus*) of another. One need only keep track of the

frequency with which words compounded from *fur* ("thief") occur in these poems to recognize that the pose of the elegiac lover is not that of a respectable figure in society. Thus, the IRONY of Tibullus's craving the social recognition of a figure like Messalla when striking such a pose is doubly rich. One of the questions that recurs in elegiac criticism is how are we to interpret that irony. Is it self-deflating humor, direct satire, or an expected part of the elegiac form? As is often the case in literary matters and particularly in elegy, these are not mutually exclusive alternatives.

Lastly, the *dominus difficilis* who keeps Delia under lock and key represents another stock figure from the world of elegy, the *diues amator*, or "wealthy lover." The *diues amator* is precisely someone who adopts the style of life Tibullus rejects in the first fifty lines of 1.1. He is the seafaring merchant, the freebooting soldier, for whom no danger, no crime is too great, so long as it brings wealth. The *diues amator*, thus, in contrast to the humble servant of the Muses, is one who is able to support a *meretrix* like Delia in the style to which she hopes to become accustomed. Of course, in so far as Tibullus was in reality an equestrian, and thus possessed a net worth of at least 500,000 sesterces, and in so far as he had gone on campaign with Messalla, then the supposed opposition between the *pauper poeta* and the *diues amator* would have brought a knowing smile to the ancient reader's lips.

Yet poem 1.2 is not a straightforward serenade by a locked out lover. We open *in medias res* in a typically Tibullan dreamlike situation. The poet is calling for more wine. He hopes to drink himself to sleep and forget his heartbreak. Yet where exactly is he? Who is to bring him more wine, and where does he propose to lay his head in a drunken stupor? Perhaps, the whole poem is a drunken fantasy, and the poet is in a bar or at a drinking party. A few lines later, however, he is clearly portrayed as the *exclusus amator* standing before Delia's door where she is kept under strict guard. From a logical point of view, it is hard to imagine how both settings can be actual, unless the whole scene transpires within the poet's head. This confusion of location has given rise to much debate. Scholars have tried to prove he is "really" at a drinking party, before Delia's door with a train of slaves, or drunk in a tavern.

Nonetheless, the central question is not what is the situation portrayed in the poem—whether real, imagined, experienced, recalled, or dreamed—but what does it mean to create poetry capable of being read in such contradictory ways? To insist on a single meaning is to apply a standard alien to Tibullus's text and its time. Elegy was never meant to be confessional poetry but a rhetorical and artistic artifact. The seeming contradictions are not flaws but the poem's subject matter in the deepest sense. They are why we continue to read and reread these poems long after straightforward expressions of emotion would have ceased to draw our attention. The story of my neighbor's divorce or of your brother's indiscretion is simply not that interesting. Elegiac poetry depends less on the accurate imitation of life than on a set of conventions that make possible its aesthetic framing, and hence potential universalization, while simultaneously insisting on the irreducible particularity of desire: Delia is the only love for me. This is the elegiac paradox.

1–2   The poet calls for unmixed wine (*merum*) to drown his sorrows in drunken sleep. The Romans considered it uncouth to drink wine that was not mixed with water.

adde and **compesce** = imperatives. The force of the commands forms an IRONIC contrast to the poet's helplessness.

occupet = subjunctive in a purpose clause

3–4   **percussum** Supply *me*.

tempora = a Greek accusative of respect

excitet = jussive subjunctive. Observe the transformation from a purpose clause in the previous couplet to a mild command. The poet's tone alternates between the imperious and the wheedling.

Note the emphatic final position of *amor*.

5–6   Only now is mention made of the beloved's locked door. Are we to imagine this scene taking place before it? Or given the emphasis on sleep, dreams, and drunken oblivion, should we rather assume that the whole scene plays out in the poet's befogged mind? For more on this and the following lines, see the "Introduction."

In opposition to the previous emphasis on sleep and rest, here we have words that indicate firmness, opposition, and traditional masculine military virtues (*saeua, dura, firma*), qualities ironically transferred to the door and, by implication, to Delia.

7–8   As often in a paraclausithyron, the poet directly addresses the door. He begins with threats.

difficilis = an *ex commune* construction, vocative with *ianua*, gen. with *domini*

uerberet and **petant** = jussive subjunctives. Jupiter as the father of the daylight sky (*Diespiter*) was the god who sent rain and storms.

9–10   When the door does not yield to his initial threats, the poet quickly changes tactics and prays the door will yield to his complaints (*querellis*).

Note the repetition of *ianua* at the beginning of two consecutive couplets. This is an example of the rhetorical figure of ANAPHORA, which is common in Tibullus (Fineberg 1991: 57–58). It is reinforced by both the additional *ianua* in line 6 and the immediately following *iam* in **9**. Final *m*'s were commonly nasalized in Latin, so that for the person reading aloud or listening the initial impression would be that the poet was beginning yet another repetition of the same word.

pateas and **sones** = jussive subjunctives

uni mihi = " for me alone"; the poet worries that the door might open for his rivals as well.

uicta recalls *lumina uicta* in **2**. Note the use of military metaphors.

furtim = literally in the manner of a *fur* or "thief." The poet/lover seeks to take what belongs to the *dominus*, Delia's love.

11–12   The poet now comically moves from his initial threats and subsequent prayers to abject apology as he recognizes the door's power to grant or deny his wishes.

mala = substantive

si qua *si* + *quis, quid* = *si aliquis, aliquid*

ignoscas = yet another jussive subjunctive. As in poem 1.1, the predominance of the subjunctive mood subtly emphasizes the unreality of the poet's fantasy.

sint precor As Perrelli observes (2002), this is an example of a PARATACTIC CONSTRUCTION. *Precor* is effectively parenthetical and the expected *ut* is omitted.

13–14　In the manner of a traditional prayer to a deity, the poet recalls his past offerings to the door in return for which he hopes his prayers will be granted (*do ut des*). This concludes the address to the door.

meminisse is a defective verb, existing only in the pf.

plurima = substantive

15–16　Tibullus begins two successive couplets with different cases of the pron. *tu*, thereby combining ANAPHORA with POLYPTOTON, the deliberate juxtaposition of different cases of the same word. Moreover, where the *te* of **13** refers to the *ianua*, the *tu* of **15** refers to Delia. Hence, this complex, double figure is used to indicate a division in poetic structure as the poet changes addressees. Lines **15–42** focus on Venus's aid to lovers.

Delia is urged to deceive her guards. Note the switch from the milder subjunctive to the imperative (*falle*), reinforced with the pass. periphrastic (*audendum est*).

adiuuat The first indicative verb in the poem is, in fact, just another form of wish fulfillment.

17–18　Tibullus begins a litany of Venus's benefactions to lovers, marked in the first instance by the ANAPHORIC use of *illa* in the next three couplets.

iuuenis For the Romans, love was the province of the young.

seu = *siue. si* + *quis, quid* = *si aliquis, aliquid*.

fixo < *figo, -ere*

dente SYNECDOCHE for key, the "teeth" of the key, for the key itself. In the elegiac scenario, the *puella* is always presumed to be locked away. There is no role for legitimate love. Love is properly thievery, the taking of another's property, whether that other be a father, a husband, a rival, a pimp, or a madam.

19-20   Venus in the next two couplets assumes the traditional elegiac role of *praeceptor amoris*.

furtim See on lines 9–10.

derepere fits the sense nicely, but is in fact only found in a late anthology. All the best manuscripts have the more prosaic *decedere*, "to move away from, leave." But it is easier to see how the rare *derepere* would be regularized to the common *decedere* in the manuscript tradition, than the other way around, although the case is far from conclusive.

21-22   **uiro** often = "husband." This would explain the presence of the *custodes*. Yet Delia in other poems seems to act much more like a *meretrix* or courtesan, in which case the *uir* would more likely be the lover who currently has a claim on Delia's affections, presumably owing to his economic investment.

conferre and **abdere** depend on *docet* in line **19**.

nutus . . . loquaces The topic of lovers' secret signs was an elegiac favorite. Ovid in *Amores* 1.4 devotes an entire poem to this topic. Note the OXYMORON of "speaking nods," as *coram* replaces *furtim*.

compositis . . . notis here = "agreed upon signs," abl. of means

23-24   Venus helps only the *fortes* (line **16**).

hoc = abl. of instrument instead of the expected double acc. (cf. Gildersleeve and Lodge ¶ 399r2)

inertia A virtue in **1.1.5** and **1.1.58**, it here becomes a vice. Superficially this aligns Tibullus with the dominant Roman ideology. But where in traditional ideology *inertia* is stigmatized because it symbolizes the opposite of the virtues of the traditional Roman farmer-soldier—courage, hard work—here it is condemned because it symbolizes the opposite of the virtues of the enterprising lover. He too must be brave and untiring but in the pursuit of a love that rightfully belongs to another, that is to say, in the pursuit of vice.

The repetition of *docet* from line **19** continues and varies the ANAPHORIC pattern.

25–26 In the best codices, lines 25 and 27 follow each other without a break. This is a metrical impossibility. Many of the lesser codices feature various conjectures for the missing line, but there is no agreement between them and none are completely convincing. Postgate's OCT labels line 27 "25a" and renumbers the lines from there. We have, however, followed the consensus numbering of modern editors.

"The juxtaposition of *vagor* and *anxius* is a typically Tibullan wordplay. *Vagor* means to 'wander about' while *anxius* is related to *ango*, 'bind' or 'choke'" (Putnam 1973).

27–28 The Roman street at night was a dangerous place since there was no formal police force. The subject of *sinit* is still Venus.

Understand *me* as the object of *occurrat*, which = final subjunctive without *ut*, a poetic construction with *sinit*.

The image of the naked poet (**rapta . . . ueste**) as the victim of a nocturnal mugger is comic.

29–30 The lover travels under divine protection. Horace treats the same theme in *Odes* 1.22, "*Integer uitae*." This summary couplet draws to a close the section on Venus's protection of illicit love.

timuisse = pf. infinitive for pres.

31–32 The scene returns to Delia's threshold. The lover is not harmed by the forces he had called down upon the recalcitrant door (7–8).

nocent . . . noctis note the pseudo-etymological wordplay. In the ancient world, as Isidorus (*Orig.* 5.31.1) tells us, *nox* was thought to be derived from *noceo*, because night is the time when harm comes to us. In fact, the words are unrelated.

33-34   Observe the ANAPHORA: three consecutive lines begin with
         non (**32, 33, 34**). This figure not only picks up on the earlier
         non in **30** but also on the repetition of *nec* in **23** (twice), **24**,
         and **27**, and the coming repetition of *neu* (**37** and **38**).

         Love here becomes *labor* (compare **1.1.3**), as the poet contin-
         ues the elegiac transvaluation of all values. Vice (illicit *amor*)
         is evaluated in terms of socially sanctioned virtue (*labor*).
         Compare *inertia* in 23.

         reseret modo Delia . . . et uocet we return to the fantasy world
         of the jussive subjunctive, "only let Delia unlock and call."

         ad . . . sonum note the HYPERBATON or disturbance of normal
         word order as the preposition is separated from its object.

         taciturna modifies *Delia*. Observe the OXYMORONIC effect of
         its juxtaposition with *sonum*. Compare **21** *nutus . . . loquaces*.

35-36   "**Parcite luminibus** could be addressed to the slaves who are
         carrying torches and accompanying the lover on his late-night
         rendezvous. 'Whether a man or a woman should be met on the
         road, spare the lights.' Although the gnomic quality of the state-
         ment could make it a general statement of amorous wisdom ad-
         dressed by the *praeceptor amoris* to his pupils. As noted above,
         this poem has no one setting nor a single addressee. The more
         common reading translates *parcite luminibus* as 'avert your
         eyes,' citing *parce oculis* in Propertius 4.9.53. The addressee then
         becomes a generic 'you.' *Lumina*, while it refers to 'eyes' in line
         2, clearly means 'torches' in **38**, just two lines later. A shift in
         meanings from one couplet to the next would be harsh, but the
         repetition of the same meaning without alteration would be oti-
         ose. Either alternative is problematic. The ambiguity, however, is
         purposeful. Love's thievery prospers in the dark, and we should
         avert our eyes since lovers are protected by Venus" (Miller 2002).

         fiat The switch from second to the impers. third person can
         seem harsh, and probably accounts for the prominence of *fias*
         in the later codices, but the switch from pl. to sing. is equally
         harsh, unless we assume that *parcite* is in fact addressed to the
         poet's accompanying slaves.

furta See on **10** and **19**.

37-38 Note the ANAPHORIC use of *neu* combined with the ALLIT-
ERATIVE *f* at the beginning of *fulgenti . . . ferte face*.

strepitu = abl. of cause

face = poetic sing. for pl.

39-40 If anyone will have been so foolish as to look, let him hide
what he sees. A future-more-vivid condition, with jussive subjunctives in the apodosis.

per . . . deos omnes a strong oath

41-42 "Whoever is talkative will know that Venus is born from
blood and the foaming sea." This allusion to Venus's birth
from the foam and blood of Uranus's testicles, when cut off
and tossed into the sea by Saturn, makes a vivid threat.

sanguine = abl. of origin.

rapido . . . mari compare Catullus 70.3–4, "mulier cupido
quod dicit amanti,/ in uento et *rapida* scribere oportet *aqua*"
("what a woman says to a desirous love ought to be written on the wind and swift water"). Tibullus rewrites Catullus's famous image of love's deceptive nature as unmanning
violence.

43-44 In a hilarious double take, Tibullus reminds us that this entire
discourse is designed to persuade a mistress who under all
constructions is not present to hear him. She is either behind
the door or a figment of his wine-sodden imagination. "But
even if someone tells your man what he has seen, I have ac-
quired a charm that insures he won't be believed." Venus may
help those who help themselves, but if not there's always black
magic. The next twenty lines are given over to the topic of
witchcraft as the poet, almost imperceptibly, modulates his
discourse from the praise of Venus to the dark world of folk
magic.

huic = *quicumque loquax* in **41**

coniunx = "spouse," but can refer to anyone with whom a
woman has a long-term and exclusive relationship

saga The wise woman is a common figure of elegy (see **1.5.59** and Propertius 1.1.19–24.), where she often doubles for the *lena* as a blocking figure in the realization of the lover's desires. Here she, at least initially, figures as his auxiliary. Love charms were a common part of ancient folk tradition and many examples of prayers and spells survive.

uerax Note how this rare word immediately casts the *saga* as someone who normally would not be presumed to speak the truth and so makes us question Tibullus's motives in making these assertions.

45–46 These proofs of the witch's power are standard. Compare Propertius 1.1.23f. The specious claim to being an eyewitness adds a touch of pathetic humor.

Note the POLYPTOTON in *hanc . . . haec.*

47–48 The ultimate proof of magical power is the ability to raise the dead.

finditque solum manesque sepulcris/ elicit = "both cleaves the soil and conjures the spirits of the dead from their graves."

49–50 The recitation of her supposed feats reaches a climax in this and the next two couplets with the assertion that she can control the spirits of the dead, the weather, and is the equal of Medea and Hecate. The climax is marked by the ANAPHORIC repetition of *iam* in this couplet, and then *cum libet* and *sola* in the next two.

stridore = a screeching like that of an owl, abl. of means. The witch's magic cry even binds the dead. The word is ONOMATOPOETIC.

aspersas lacte the dead are summoned with offerings of milk, honey, and blood. Compare the visit to the underworld in *Odyssey* 11.

referre pedem = an idiom, "to return"

51–52 **cum libet** is IRONIC. On the one hand, from the speaker's point of view, it signals the power of the witch and hence the poet as well as Delia's ability to rely upon her. This should be a means of persuasion. On the other, it signifies the absolute power of the *saga*, and hence the poet's helplessness to control her. Lastly, the association of absolute power with the desire of its holder is the ultimate erotic fantasy of every elegist.

aestiuo . . . orbe = "summer sky"

53–54   **dicitur** "we have now left the realm of 'eyewitness' reporting and are dealing with hearsay as the poet's claims to credibility are progressively weakened" (Miller 2002).

Medea's magical powers were central to Jason's acquisition of the Golden Fleece and his subsequent escape. Her skill with plants and herbs are a recurring theme in ancient literature. See Propertius 1.1.24. But given the results of Jason's love for Medea— the death of her father and brother and the murder of her and Jason's children—Delia might well question how much trust she should put in such a figure.

Hecate was the underworld aspect of the triform goddess, Artemis, Luna, Hecate. She was associated with crossroads (*triuia*) and appeared on earth accompanied by vicious dogs.

55–56   The poet arrives at his true point. The witch has given him a charm that will make him invisible to Delia's *coniunx*, so she should open her door. This whole series has been nothing more than a series of rhetorical amplifications designed to convince the mistress to satisfy his desires and hence they are completely untrustworthy.

quīs = *quibus*

fallere Understand *hunc*.

ter . . . ter The number three is common in magic.

57–58   "Even if he catches us red-handed, he won't believe his eyes."

molli . . . toro Compare *molli lecto* (**19**).

59–60   The poet suddenly realizes that if he is invisible, then his rivals might be as well. He beats a hasty retreat. The charm only works for Tibullus!

"The ENJAMBMENT of *omnia* and the splitting of the last clause by the caesura in the pentameter gives the couplet a jerky rhythm reminiscent of hasty improvisation" (Miller 2002).

abstineas We return to the jussive subjunctive.

61–62   The poet quickly tries to improvise a justification for the ridiculous position he finds himself in and piles absurdity on absurdity. He *knows* the witch can be trusted because she said she would make him fall out of love! Note the cinematic quality of these lines. We seem to watch the poet tying himself into rhetorical knots in real time.

Some editors place a comma (Perelli, and Lenz and Galinsky) or question mark (Luck, Putnam) after *quid* to make the poet's doubts in the power of magic more explicit. But this ruins much of the humor. It should be remembered that all such punctuation is postclassical.

63–64   The failed attempt to release the poet from the bonds of love is recounted.

taedis Torches were often coated with sulfur pitch, which was used in rites of purification.

nocte serena i.e., lit by the moon

ad magicos hostia pulla deos The gods of the underworld, who were appealed to in magic, received dark victims according to the principles of sympathetic magic.

65–66   The failure of the ceremony was not the *saga*'s fault, but the poet's. He prayed for eternal and mutual love, not release from its bonds. If Delia opens her door, she'll prove the efficacy of the poet's prayers and the witch's powers. This couplet serves as a coda on the *saga* section of the poem.

abesset ... esset ... uelim impf. subjunctives of indirect command after *orabam*

67–80   In the next section, the poet contrasts himself with his rival. Where the latter adopts the lifestyle of the freebooting solider, the poet now reverts to the rural fantasy that characterized **1.1**. Yet we know from the poet's own story, recounted in 1.3, that from a dramatic point of view he fits this characterization at least as much as his rival does (Putnam). Furthermore, the poet's audience would have been able to savor the IRONY of knowing that Tibullus, the person, as opposed to his poetic persona, was a wealthy equestrian who had gone on campaign with Messalla. Thus, this next section functions on three levels simultaneously: (1) It is an attack on the poet's rival for his greed and heartlessness as opposed to the poet's espousal of simple rural virtue (a position hard to square with his being drunk in the city); (2) It serves as a statement of implicit regret for the poet himself having at one point chosen the lifestyle he now attacks; (3) It opens an IRONIC metanarrative, as the poet's own lifestyle is seen to undercut the claims of his persona. Yet the fictive world also expresses a utopian critique of the poet's actual existence, so that the real and fictive each come to relativize the claims of the other.

67–68 **ille** = in the first instance, the *coniunx*

maluerit pf. subjunctive in a rel. clause of characteristic

69–70 The *coniunx* may win military glory! Note the harsh ALLIT-ERATIVE *c*'s.

Cilicum = a reference to Messalla's eastern campaign in 30–29 BCE (see 1.7.16), which would be the occasion for the opening of 1.3. The Cilicians were a people of Asia Minor involved in piracy.

ante = adverbial

Martia = not simply "military," but specifically "Roman"

71–72 As in the opening of 1.1, the corollary of military glory is monetary reward.

argento . . . auro ablatives of material. Note how the man of iron in **65** is transformed into gold and silver. The IRONY is re-inforced when we recall that the *Golden* Age was traditionally characterized by the lack of property, possessions, and hence money or exchange, while the *Iron* Age is that of greed, commerce, and an increasingly monetarized existence. See **2.3.35**.

conspiciendus = "striking"

73-76   The contrast between the lives of *ille* and *ipse* is given added point by having the former described in a series of affirmative declarations dependent on *licet*, whereas the vision of latter is described in a future-less-vivid condition (*si . . . possim . . . liceat*). The grammar tells the story. *Ille* lives in the world of actuality, *ipse* in that of desire.

73-74   **mea . . . Delia** = vocative

boues . . . iungere = to hitch oxen to the plough

75-76   Note the way in which *retinere lacertis* recapitulates the letters in *liceat teneris*.

mollis = predicative. Sleep will be "soft" with Delia, even on the raw earth.

Note the feminine gender of *humo*.

77-78   While ostensibly continuing the contrast between *ipse* and *ille*, there is no hint in the Tibullan corpus that Delia's *coniunx* plays the elegiac lover and weeps in a sleepless bed. This experience would appear to be the poet's alone, reinforcing Putnam's reading that *ille* represent less a separate person than an aspect of the poet's existence from which the elegiac lover has become alienated.

Tyrio . . . toro The reference is to purple dyed coverlets, a sign of luxury.

79-80   Luxury is of no avail in combating the insomnia of the loveless. Note the ALLITERATION of *nam neque . . . nec . . . nec*.

plumae = soft, feather pillows and mattresses

stragula picta = richly embroidered spreads

placidae . . . aquae = a fountain in a wealthy house. The sound of running water is, to this day, considered by many to be an aid to sleep.

81-88   The poet reflects on the possible causes of his misfortune.

81-82   "Have I violated the godhead of Venus?" Venus is often METONYMY for love, and it could well be Delia who has been angered and, as a consequence, locked him out (Putnam, Perrelli).

num Do not translate.

83–84 Observe the ANAPHORA with *num*. Note how it echoes *nam* in **79–80**, creating a rhetorical linkage and smoothing the transition from one section of the poem to the next. It also anticipates the repetition of *non* in **85–86** and **87–88**.

feror = "I am said"

incestus = the negative of *castus*

serta Would these be the same garlands he hung on Delia's door in **14**?

85–86 The poet proclaims his eagerness for self-abasement. The possibility of an erotic double entendre is not to be ruled out in the image of the poet on his hands and knees kissing the threshold to the temple of Venus.

87–88 The poet had adopted the position of a suppliant (*supplex*) in relation to Delia's door in **14**. Compare **1.1.73–74**'s *frangere postes/ non pudet*.

89–98 The poem concludes with a series of threats against those who would mock the ill-fated lover. The passage recapitulates the poem's second theme by demonstrating the powers of Venus.

89–90 "Laugh while you may, it'll be your turn soon!"

The direct address of a *tu* once more poses the question of the setting of the poem. It could be a generalized *tu*, although then we might more logically expect the pl. It could be a passerby such as was warned away in **35–42** or a fellow drinker. There is no overriding reason why these ambiguities need to be resolved.

caueto = fut. imperative

91–92 Those who mock love when they are young often become elderly suitors, a figure of fun in elegy (see **1.1.72**) and comedy.

uidi ego The credibility of this claim is in fact no higher than that found for the same phrase in **45**.

The antecedent of *qui* = *senem*, which is the subject of the infinitive after a verb of perception.

lusisset plpf. subjunctive in a rel. clause of characteristic. The phrase is common in comedy.

93-94 The elderly suitor trying to comb his sparse gray hairs with his fingers is a prime example of Tibullan comic pathos.

95-96 It does not shame the suitor to play a part inappropriate for his age. Compare Catullus 5.2, "rumoresque senum seueriorum."

ancillam The maid in comedy and elegy often serves as go-between for illicit lovers. The old man is so shameless as to detain her in the middle of the forum.

97-98 The elderly suitor becomes a figure of fear and mockery among the young. The repetition of *hunc* is emphatic.

circumterit occurs only here in extant Latin and may be a Tibullan coinage. The image is vivid. The crowd of young men and boys surrounds the elderly suitor, jostling and rubbing against him in a kind of scrum.

despuit Compare **56**. Spitting is a common part of apotropaic magic. The old man is a monstrosity. The youths spit in their togas to avoid any possible contagion. Such practices were common at the sight of madmen and epileptics.

99-100 A final prayer to Venus: the agricultural motif returns, as the poet asks why the goddess would burn her own harvest. But from the evidence of the poem, the prayer is too late.

∿ 1.4

Priapus introduces the standard elegiac figure of the *praeceptor amoris* in this poem that looks back to the pederastic content of Hellenistic elegy. This poem has often been neglected. It is not hard to understand why. It features a speaker who is represented as either having or being a giant penis and gives advice on how to pick up boys. Yet, to ignore this poem is to ignore much of what separates the ancient world from our own. Homoerotic liaisons between older men and adolescents were an accepted part of ancient life, and many of the conventions of heteroerotic elegy make their first appearance in Greek pederastic poetry.

The poem itself is largely a comical exercise. It opens with the poet beseeching Priapus to share the secrets of his erotic success. The central portion is a speech by the god himself, envisioned as a garden scarecrow, using comically inflated language. We return to the poet's voice in the last twelve lines where he first celebrates his status as the transmitter of the god's lessons, only to reveal their utter failure in the case of his love for Marathus (see also **1.9**).

Talking objects were not in themselves unusual in poetry. Hellenistic epigram featured many cult statues and tombs that hailed passersby in elegiac couplets. Elegy was the preferred meter of epigrams, which had themselves originated as metrical inscriptions on objects. In Latin, precedent

Fig. 1. Priapus was a phallic god endowed with fertility. Mid-second century CE marble statue. Cortile del Belvedere, Museo Pio Clementino, Vatican Museums.Vanni / Art Resource, NY

for such talking objects could be found in Catullus. Poem 4 in iambic senarii, for example, features a garrulous yacht describing its journey from Asia Minor to Lake Garda. Catullus 66 is a metrical translation of Callimachus's "Lock of Berenice," in which the lock of hair explains its transformation into a constellation. Finally, Catullus 67 is a kind of reverse paraclausithyron, again in elegiac couplets. In it, the poet solicits a door to tell the speaker of the sexual shenanigans that took place behind it. In Tibullus 1.4, the poet asks the statue to reveal to him his secrets for attracting beautiful boys. The statue in turn takes on one of the most common roles in the elegiac scenario, that of *praeceptor amoris* or "love tutor." This is normally a comic role, which was most famously embodied in Ovid's three-book didactic parody, the *Ars Amatoria* or *Art of Love*.

The poet concedes from the beginning that Priapus seems a most unlikely Don Juan. He stands naked and unkempt, exposed to the elements, hardly the image of suave sophistication. Of course part of the joke is that statues of the god were always portrayed either as being or having a giant erect penis. Priapus is raw desire. If anyone should know the secret, it's him. Yet the god answers the poet's query with a lengthy and pretentious speech, filled with rhetorical niceties. The utter disproportion between his rhetoric and his appearance is a primary source of the poem's humor. Priapus's speech itself features many of the same motifs that are found in heteroerotic elegy, most prominently a lengthy tirade against the elegiac lover's arch nemesis, the *diues amator*:

> heu male nunc artes miseras haec saecula tractant:
>   iam tener adsueuit munera uelle puer.
> at tua, qui uenerem docuisti uendere primus,
>   quisquis es, infelix urgeat ossa lapis.   60
> Pieridas, pueri, doctos et amate poetas,
>   aurea nec superent munera Pieridas. (1.4.57–62)

The arch language and the over-the-top defense of the desire of poets momentarily and ironically lets the mask slip, revealing the phallic god's plea for young boys to yield to poets as humorously self-serving. Yet it is also ultimately ineffectual if not to say impotent. This speech, the poet tells us at the end of the poem, which he heard and now transmits to others, has made him the toast of the town and established his own reputation as a *praeceptor amoris*, but alas (*eheu*) Marathus still tortures him in love, and his arts are of no avail (1.4.81–82).

1–2   The poet seeks the favor of Priapus, whose statue often served as a scarecrow in fields and gardens, by wishing that it be protected from the elements.

contingant . . . noceantque = jussive subjunctives

3–4   Can he explain his success with beautiful boys? It's certainly not owed to his personal grooming.

sollertia here = Greek *technē*

5–6   The repetition of *nudus* is IRONIC. On the one hand, it acknowledges the god's lack of refinement (*non tibi culta*) and his rustic nature, since he must endure the elements without even elemental shelter. On the other, it recognizes his sexual power.

brumae = literally, the shortest day of the year (*breuima*), the solstice. Naked Priapus, thus, lengthens (*producis*) "the shortest." The obscene etymological pun signals the nature of what is to follow. *Produco*, of course, also means "endure."

Canis See on **1.1.27**.

7–8   This transitional couplet prepares us for the central portion of the poem, which consists of Priapus's speech on how to seduce.

sic ego = a standard epic transition between speeches found in Homer and Vergil, here clearly IRONIC

Bacchi . . . proles Priapus was the son of Bacchus. *Proles* = mock epic diction.

9–10   "Do not entrust yourself to the crowd of boys, for they always give good cause to fall in love."

fuge . . . credere The combination of the imperative with the explanatory infinitive is heightened poetic diction, comic in the mouth of a naked phallic deity.

11–12   Priapus begins a list of different kinds of boys and their various charms.

The image of the youth pushing back the water with a "snowy chest" (*niueo pectore*) is striking. Paleness is normally a mark of effeminacy, at odds with the masculine strength on display.

13–14   Both the forward and the shy attract.

15–16   But even if at first they play coy, persistence pays in the end.

capiant = jussive subjunctive with *taedia* as subject

negabit . . . dabit Assume *puer* as subject.

sub iuga colla dabit a standard image of willing subjection to another

17-18 Note how the ANAPHORA of *longa dies* here and *annus* in the next couplet mimics the repetitive nature of the processes offered in evidence to support Priapus's position.

longa = "many a"

leones and **saxa** The paradox of the most fierce of animals rendered docile and of hard stone consumed by soft water humorously dramatizes the difficulty of the would-be pederast's task.

19-20 **certa . . . uice** an OXYMORON. Change in the Roman mind is normally the opposite of certainty.

lucida signa = the signs of the zodiac

21-26 Lover's oaths were thought not to reach the gods' ears and hence to be unreliable.

21-22 Compare the famous image in Catullus 70.

freta = SYNECDOCHE (part for the whole) for sea

summa = superl. of *superus*

23-24 **gratia magna Ioui** = "great thanks be to Jove." As the philanderer in chief, Jupiter, who normally enforces oaths, becomes the patron of perjury.

25-26 The IRONY of two virgin goddesses allowing you to swear falsely in love increases the humor.

sinit . . . adfirmes poetic construction without *ut*. Compare **1.2.27–28**.

Dictynna = "the lady of the net," a cult title for Diana as goddess of the hunt, hence swearing by her "arrows"

Minerua was especially proud of her hair.

27-28 After earlier counseling patience, Priapus now recommends speed.

The final syllable of *eris* is lengthened before the caesura. See Maltby on the prosody of this passage.

29–30 Note the ANAPHORIC repetition. *Colores* = a common METON-YMY for flowers.

deperdit is understood with *populus* as well.

31–32 **quam** = *quam cito*. Perrelli (2002) notes the phonological re-semblance between *quam cito* and *quam iacet*, while observ-ing that *iacet* effectively means the opposite of *cito*.

uenere = 3rd pl. pf.

prior is attributive and has an essentially adverbial force, "before."

Eleo the Olympic games were held at Elis in the Pelopenese. The old racehorse has reached his retirement.

carcere = the starting gate

33–34 The truism of age regretting a misspent youth here becomes an admonition to undertake the labors of pederasty quickly. In this upside down world, erotic pursuits are matters of high seriousness.

maerentem modifies *iuuenem*.

stultos = "foolish," hence "wasted"

35–36 The snake may shed its skin each year, but beauty merely ages.

crudeles diui! Priapus, of course, is a god too, even if not a very glamorous one.

dedere = 3rd pl. pf. < *do*

37–38 The gods alone have eternal youth. Bacchus and Apollo bal-ance the earlier pair of Diana and Minerva.

intonsus crinis Uncut hair is a sign of youth and hence often of erotic availability.

39–52 This section is devoted to *seruitium amoris*. Whether in ho-moerotic or heteroerotic poetry, the formula is the same. The socially superior lover (i.e., older male) subjects himself to his social inferior (younger male or female) in hopes of receiving erotic compensation. The humor of the superior performing servile tasks was part of the charm.

39–40 **cedas** = jussive subjunctive

obsequio plurima uincet amor an IRONIC recasting of *Eclogues* 10.69, *omnia uincit amor*

41–42　Where long journeys are normally rejected in Tibullus, as signs of greed and the end of the Golden Age, Priapus here counsels the opposite: go wherever the boy leads.

paretur = pres. pass. subjunctive with *quamuis*

Canis see on **1.1.27.**

43–44　This is a very difficult couplet that has given rise to much interpretive controversy and numerous textual emendations. The text printed here is that of the vulgate, with one change. *Admittat*, found in some of the later mss., has been substituted for the unmetrical *amiciat*. The acceptance of this reading involves lengthening the final short syllable before the caesura, an uncommon but not unprecedented practice in Tibullus and the poets of this period. See *eris* in **27**. For more, see the discussions in Putnam (1973), Perrelli (2002), and Maltby (2002).

The rainbow in the classical world was a sign of storms to come not of their end, as in Hebrew texts. Thus the rainbow is *imbrifer* and fringes (*praetexens*) the sky with the painted purple (*picta ferrugine*) of storm clouds.

45–46　The image of a Roman equestrian rowing his beloved across the sea is a moment of inspired comedy.

puppi = a common SYNECDOCHE for the ship as a whole

47–48　Compare this couplet to **1.1.29–30**, both in terms of content and the use of pf. infinitives (*subiisse, atteruisse*) for the pres.

paeniteat = jussive subjunctive

insuetas . . . manus Callused hands are the sign of manual labor. The poet's are tender.

opera = abl. of means

atteruisse = archaic for *attriuisse* < *attero*. "Another example of the preciosity of Priapus's language" (Maltby 2002).

49–50   In ancient hunts, slaves closed off a valley with nets to trap the prey. Again the emphasis is on the putative social superior performing servile manual labor.

As Perrelli notes (2002), the extreme HYPERBATON and EN-JAMBMENT (continuation of sense across the metrical break) separating *nec* from *negent*, in combination with the double negative, is unexampled elsewhere in Tibullan verse and makes for very refined poetic language.

dum placeas = "provided that you would be pleasing [to him]"

51–52   If he wishes to fence, let him win!

dextra Understand *manus.*

The sexual double entendre of *nudum . . . latus* need hardly be pointed out.

53–54   By making yourself subservient, he in turn will make himself vulnerable, and you can take what you desire.

Implied violence is a constant feature of ancient hetero- and homoerotic discourse. It is summed up in the paradox of *rapta dabit.*

55–56   At first he will yield. Then, he will come of his own accord.

adferet Assume *oscula* as object.

se implicuisse "The elision of the caesura is purposeful. The prosody enacts inseparability of the beloved from the lover" (Miller 2002).

57–70   A common complaint of the elegiac lover: in these fallen times, love is for sale. The *diues amator* is the poet's nemesis.

57–58   **artes miseras** It is not till the following line that we realize that these "arts" refer to trading love for gifts, not *seruitium amoris.* On this and the following line, see the "Introduction."

saecula The fall from a past Golden Age is a recurrent theme is Tibullus.

59–60   A curse on the first teacher of mercenary love. Let him not rest in peace.

61-62 Love the Muses and their devotees!

Pieridas the Muses of Pieria, an area in Thessaly. Zeus was their father.

doctos a common neoteric and later Augustan epithet for poetry and poets

63-64 Poetry is what makes myth immortal.

purpurea ... Nisi coma Nisus was king of Megara. His kingdom's safety depended on the existence of a single purple hair. His daughter, Scylla, cut it off for love of Minos, king of Crete.

ex umero Pelopis ... ebur Pelops was served by his father, Tantalus, to the gods. When they realized, they refused the meal. Demeter, however, had already swallowed his shoulder. Jupiter replaced it with ivory. Tantalus was condemned to hunger and thirst in Hades.

65-66 **uehet** is the verb for all three *dum* clauses.

67-70 An elaborate curse, let him who sells love for money become a follower of the Great Mother goddess, Cybele. Cybele's priests underwent a ritual castration. See the story recounted in Catullus 63.

audit = "heed"

Idaeae Cybele's home was on Mt. Ida.

currus poetic pl. Cybele's chariot was drawn by lions.

sequatur, expleat, secet = jussive subjunctives

Opis the Roman goddess of plenty, often assimilated to Phrygian Cybele

tercentenas an indefinitely large number

Phrygios ... modos The Phrygian mode was thought to inspire ecstatic and irresponsible behavior, hence Plato's proposal to ban it in the *Republic*.

71-72 A final summary: Venus favors the traditional topics of the elegiac poet: flattery, tears, and complaints.

locum = "occasion"

querellis/supplicibus, miseris fletibus Note the use of EN-JAMBMENT and ASYNDETON, the lack of an expected conj., to heighten the diction and mark this couplet as concluding the central section of the poem.

73–84 Priapus's speech is at an end, and what we thought was direct is now revealed to have been reported speech. The poet assumes the standard elegiac role of *praeceptor amoris*. Yet, the comic element continues. He is a failure, in the first instance, because the otherwise unknown Titius's wife will not let the latter learn the lessons the poet transmits and, in the second, because the poet is tortured by his unrequited love for Marathus.

73–74 **canerem** rel. clause of purpose

edidit ore an epic phrase often used of oracles

75–76 Titius can have his wife. I am the toast of all those whom boys torment.

pareat jussive subjunctive

suae = substantive

male habet an idiom, "to have in a bad way"

77–78 **gloria cuique sua est** = "to each man his own glory," perhaps proverbial

amantes = substantive use of the pple.

consultent = jussive subjunctive

ianua nostra patet The door of the *praeceptor*, unlike that of the beloved, is always open.

79–80 The poet imagines the future glory to be gained in his role as *praeceptor*, passing on the lessons he has learned from the god.

deducat a term for escorting distinguished citizens; potential subjunctive

81–82 Just when the poet imagines his greatest glory, it all comes tumbling down. His arts fail. *eheu* = *heu*, compare 57.

83–84 The poet pleads for mercy, lest he become a fable, which the publication of the poem insures.

ne . . . fiam = negative purpose clause

◌ *1.5*

Tibullus envisions his rural ideal of Delia as mistress of his farm serving the first fruits to Messalla, while acknowledging the impossibility of his dream in the famous phrase, "haec mihi fingebam." The poem begins with Tibullus standing firm and ready to call an end to the affair but his resolution melts away before the first couplet is through. The poet compares himself to a top spun now here, now there, by a group of young boys. He then proceeds to tell how he had performed certain magical rites that had saved Delia from illness only to have another enjoy the benefits. From there, we modulate into the dream sequence before returning to a comic passage in which the poet details the various failed ways he had employed to try and forget Delia. This comic interlude leads to a lengthy curse against the procuress, who had persuaded Delia to prefer money to love, and a panegyric of the poor lover. The poem ends with a warning to his wealthy rival that the wheel of Fortune turns for all and his turn is coming too.

This poem contains some of the most moving passages in the corpus: the lover driven by passion compared to a top spun by young boys (1.5.3–4), the return of the rural dream with Tibullus now as Delia's *custos* (1.5.21–22), the image of the rival lover's fortune as a boat adrift in flowing waters (1.5.76). A certain melancholy quality, which has long been recognized in Tibullan poetry, is given a particular accentuation in 1.5. Perhaps here more than anywhere the poet recognizes that the final conjugation of his desires for rural ease, the love of his mistress, and the recognition and approval of his patron is an impossible dream. This is nowhere made clearer than in the following passage, in which the poet admits that he can only imagine a form of fulfillment in which peace, ease, prosperity, love, and honor could coincide without his own active participation.

> *illa* regat cunctos, illi sint omnia curae:
> at iuuet in tota me nihil esse domo.   30
> huc ueniet Messalla meus, cui dulcia poma
> Delia selectis detrahat arboribus:

et, tantum uenerata uirum, hunc sedula curet,
    huic paret atque epulas ipsa ministra gerat.
haec mihi fingebam, quae nunc Eurusque Notusque 35
    iactat odoratos uota per Armenios. (1.5.29–36)

[Let her rule everyone, let the care of everything be
hers: and let it make me happy to be nothing in the
whole house. My Messalla will come here, for whom
let Delia draw down sweet fruits from specially chosen
trees: and having paid her respect to such a great man,
let her diligently care for him and let she herself, as
a servant, prepare and bring for him feasts fit for a
god. These things I was fabricating for myself, which
prayers now the East and South winds toss about
among the perfumed Armenians]

There are a number of elements that should be noticed about this
passage. First, Delia, here, is imagined as a true *domina*, a traditional mistress of a household, normally the owner's wife (*matrona*),
who commanded its servants. The elegiac use of the term was a later
variation, and the restoration of its original meaning is a deft poetic
move. At the same time, Delia being pictured as a *domina* is a clear
sign of the impossibility of the dream articulated in this passage: for
the idea of a freedwoman *meretrix* serving as a traditional *matrona*
on the estate of a respectable Roman farmer is *prima facie* absurd, yet
it is also the necessary condition for Tibullus's dream to be realized.

Second, we should observe the predominance of the subjunctive
mood in these lines. This is a recurrent feature of Tibullus's Latin. In
the opening couplets of 1.1, where the fantasy of rural ease is first and
most extensively elaborated, we do not have a verb in the indicative for
ten lines, and after that the subjunctive remains the poem's predomi-
nant mood. In other poems, the ratio of subjunctive to indicative verbs
may not be so extreme, but Tibullus's poetry and consequently his Latin focuses squarely on the hypothetical, the potential, and the jussive.

Third, on the one hand, this passage expresses the poet's desire.
It is from his point of view that this string of jussive subjunctives

issues (*regat, sint, iuuet, curet, paret, gerat*). On the other, part of that wish is that Tibullus be nothing in the house (*me nihil esse domo*). On the surface, this would seem to mean that he would have no part in his own affairs, that Delia would be completely dominant on the estate. This would be a very strange situation for a Roman equestrian in which to find himself in relation to a freedwoman dependent. Yet, on a more profound level, it is as though the poet wished for his own death, his own annihilation (*nihil esse*). His desire, it seems, can only be realized on the condition of his nonexistence, and indeed he plays no part in the following scene where Delia serves Messalla. Lest this be considered over reading, fantasies of the poet's death are a frequent part of elegy, often featuring elaborate imaginings of the beloved's grief at the lover's grave (see, for example, **1.1.61–70**), and may be part of the elegiac meter's traditional association with lamentation and mourning. Admittedly, all this can seem rather strange to a modern audience, but to anyone who appreciates the guilty pleasures of nineteenth-century opera or even the end of *Romeo and Juliet*, the power of such scenes and their sentiments will not be unfamiliar.

Fourth, Messalla here, who represents everything the poet does not—power, wealth, social respectability—is treated like a god. To him the lone indicative verb is attributed (*ueniet*), attaining a vividness that momentarily cuts through the gauzy fantasy structure of the scene as a whole. Delia offers him the fruits of the harvest as to an agricultural god (compare **1.1.13–24, 1.5.27–28**). She worships him (*uenerata*), and in the manner of a priestess (*ministra*) serves him a banquet like those offered at feasts celebrating the gods (*epulas*). Thus, when the dream is posited as realized, in this one moment, there is a complete coincidence of all the poet's competing desires. His beloved has left the city to run his country estate, and his patron, the image of social respectability and possessing the attributes of a god, has come and is served in perfect harmony. Rural ease, erotic fulfillment, social recognition, and traditional piety are one! Only, and it is easy to forget this, Tibullus is not there (*me nihil esse*). The possibility of his desire's fulfillment is structured around his absence.

Finally, the sudden shift to the imperfect indicative in the last couplet denotes an abrupt return to reality. *haec mihi fingebam*: "these things I was fashioning/ imagining/ making up for myself." It was all a dream, completely insubstantial, a puff of smoke, which has become the plaything of the winds among the exotic and effeminate, perfumed Armenians. The impossibility of this dream, moreover, a dream which in many ways represents a very serious articulation of traditional Roman values—the presence of the *domina/matrona*, the traditional life of the farmer, the piety of ancestral religious observances, respect for the traditional social hierarchies—says something serious about a crisis in Roman life at the end of the civil wars and the beginning of the Augustan period. These desires have not lost their power, but they are also no longer completely imaginable. At the same time, such desires also seem naïve and unsophisticated. The arch image of the poet's prayers (*uota*) as a bauble for the winds among remote, eastern perfume wearers, casts the whole scenario as an IRONIC commentary on the present and on the nostalgia for an idealized past, which was a prominent element in the propaganda of the Augustan regime. The dream itself becomes from this perspective the object of the knowing poet's cynical smile.

1–2   Note the sharp contrast between the impf. tense in hexameter and the pres. in the pentameter.

gloria fortis These terms, which would normally refer to the rewards of military bravery, are here turned first to feminized eroticism, then are said to be absent altogether. This kind of double displacement is typical of Tibullus and part of what constitutes the disorienting and "dreamlike" quality of the text.

3–4   A striking SIMILE: the poet is in a whirl, like a top driven by a young boy.

uerbere = the "blow" of the string

turben This form is very rare, and would normally be *turbo*. *Turben* is listed as neuter when quoted by the late grammarian Charisius, who vouches for the passage. Nonetheless, it here has to be m. like *turbo*.

puer The reader who had just come from **1.4** would naturally assume that this was Marathus. It is not until line **9** that we learn that the object of the poet's anxiety and desire is, once more, a woman.

5–6 The unfaithful *seruus amoris* must undergo the tortures of all runaways and learn the humility of his position.

ure imperative = to brand a runaway, normally on the face

libeat ne = negative purpose clause

7–8 A superbly IRONIC couplet. The poet pleads for mercy, citing the *furtiui foedera lecti*, *Venerem*, and Delia's *compositum caput*.

per . . . furtiui foedera lecti A *foedus* is a divinely sanctioned contract or pact. It was first used METAPHORICALLY of a love relationship by Catullus. *furtiui . . . lecti* indicates that Delia, as we have seen in **1.2**, in fact belonged to another. Hence, the entire notion of a "*foedus* of infidelity" is wildly inappropriate, a fact reinforced by Tibullus's word placement.

te = direct object of *quaeso*

per Venerem This would be a standard formula for swearing by Venus. Editors, however, hesitate on the capitalization. Most ancient texts would have been written in all capital letters. In context, the poet could be begging for mercy not only in the name of the divinity but also of his and Delia's carnal relations, *per uenerem*.

compositumque caput a brilliant anticlimax. The poet pleads in the name of their pledges of faithful infidelity, their divine carnality, and Delia's hairdo!

9–16 The poet cites as a sign of his loyalty magical rites performed when Delia was ill.

9–10 **ille ego . . . dicor** = "I am called the one who." His role is well known.

eripuisse = pf. infinitive for pres.

11–12 Note the emphatic repetition of *ipse* in this and the next two couplets.

sulpure puro Smoking sulphur was used during rites of purification. Tibullus would have walked around (*circum*) Delia with the sulphur while the rite was peformed.

praecinuisset plpf. subjunctive in the *cum* clause

13–14 **ter** a common number in magical and religious contexts

deueneranda = a rare compound, modifying *saeua . . . somnia*, used only here in the sense of "to ward off with prayers or sacrifices"

sancta . . . mola = abl. of means

15–16 Magical and religious rites in Rome were often performed with the head "covered" (*uelatus*) by a woolen fillet (*filo*). The clothing was loose with nothing knotted or tied (*solutis*).

nouem = 3x3, a powerful number in a ritual context

Triuiae = a cult title of Hecate, often identified with Diana. *Triuia* = the conjunction of three roads.

17–18 I fulfilled (*persolui*) all my vows, but now another enjoys the fruits of my labors.

fruitur and **utitur** take the abl.

19–36 The poet here articulates the full nature of his dream of rural ease: a return to a state of simplicity, Delia's presence, and the approval of Messalla. This is a world in which personal, erotic, and social fulfillment coincide. At the same time, as he acknowledges at the passage's beginning (**20**) and end (**35**), it is a fiction (*fingebam*).

19–20 Note the repetition of *felix* from the previous couplet.

salua = recovered from her illness

fuisses = plpf. subjunctive < *sum* in a past contrary-to-fact condition

renuente deo abl. absolute, "nodding back in disapproval," rather than forwards in approval

21–22 The shift to the fut. indicative makes the dream, confected in the past, a vivid, if momentary, reality.

In **1.2**, Delia is watched over by a *custos*. In Tibullus's dream, she becomes the *custos*.

area = subject.

23-24 She will guard the ideal plenty produced by his estate.

25-26 Delia becomes the typical Roman *domina*, the mistress of the household slaves, as opposed to the elegiac *domina*, mistress of the *seruus amoris*. Note how *amantis* suggests the elegiac role, even as *uerna* makes the more traditional sense clear.

Observe the repetition of *consuescet*. The change in subject does not become evident until the pentameter.

27-28 Delia here is imagined as occupying the same role as Tibullus in **1.1.13–14**.

Note the influence of sympathetic magic. An offering is made of that which the god is supposed to foster: grapes for vines; ears of grain for cereals; sacrifice for meat.

sciet . . . ferre = "will know how to bring"

29-30 "Delia as *domina* will be in charge of all. Tibullus will rejoice in doing nothing, but *esse nihil* literally means 'to be nothing.' It is as if he does not exist" (Miller 2002).

regat . . . sint = jussive subjunctives

31-32 The imaginary duo of Delia and Tibullus becomes a triangle as Messalla, the representative of Roman society, enters the dream.

detrahat = potential subjunctive

33-34 Delia will subordinate herself to Messalla as personal, erotic, and social desire momentarily become one.

There is no elision between *uirum* and *hunc* owing to the word division falling on the caesura.

huic Remember *ui* is a dipthong.

paret = jussive subjunctive < *parō*

35-36 We return the frame of the dream in which its fictive nature is acknowledged.

odoratos . . . Armenios proverbial of eastern exoticism

37–38 The return to the fallen world of reality. Note the ANAPHORIC repetition of *saepe* in this and the following couplet.

curas depellere uino Compare **1.2.1–4.**

uerterat = plpf. < *uertō*. Instead of water being turned into wine, wine is turned into tears.

39–40 Often I sought comfort in the arms of another, only to fail to rise to the occasion.

gaudia a common sexual euphemism

adirem impf. subjunctive in a *cum* clause

admonuit Assume *me.*

41–42 The new woman departs, accusing the poet of having been cursed (*deuotum*) by Delia.

meam = the subject of *scire* in indirect discourse. Assume *dominam.*

43–44 Delia does not bewitch with spells (*uerbis*) but with beauty.

hoc refers back to the fact of the poet's bewitchment.

45–46 Mythological exempla are a common in elegy, but relatively rare in Tibullus.

Nereis . . . Thetis Thetis, the mother of Achilles, was a sea nymph and daughter of Nereus. The story of her marriage to the mortal Peleus is recounted in Catullus 64.

Pelea = Greek acc.

Note the elaborate interlaced word order of the pentameter.

47–48 A transitional couplet. As in **17**, the first hemistich or "half of the line" refers back to the previous topic (the poet's bewitchment) and the rest introduces a new topic (the poet's rival). The *diues amator*, as we have already seen in **1.4.57–72**, is the elegiac poet's nemesis.

nocuere = 3rd pl. pf.

huic = Delia

callida lena a madam, hence Delia is a *meretrix*

49-50   The next three couplets are given over to an elaborate curse on the *lena*.

sanguineas ... dapes not burnt sacrifice to the gods of the upper world, but blood sacrifice to those of the underworld

edat ... bibat = jussive subjunctive

51-52   Let her be haunted by cursed spirits and dire omens.

uolitent ... canat = jussive subjunctive

strix "Ov. *Fast.* 6.131–43 describes it as an owl that screeches horribly and sucks the blood of children" (Maltby 2002).

53-54   May her hunger be such that she gnaws grass and bones from graves.

fame stimulante = abl. absolute

quaerat = jussive subjunctive

"There is a pun in *lupis. Lupa* was slang for prostitute, and hence appropriate for a *lena*" (Miller 2002).

55-56   May she be chased by dogs naked through the street. This is an image of complete abjection and humiliation.

currat ... ululet ... agat = jussive subjunctive

57-58   This curse will come to pass because lovers have divine protection.

iniusta lege The law that binds Delia and the poet is unjust because it has been broken.

59-60   The poet directly addresses Delia.

quam primum = "as soon as possible"

sagae The *lena* has now been assimilated to the figure of the witch.

desere = imperative

donis uincitur omnis amor another parody of *Eclogues* 10.69, *omnia uincit amor.* See **1.4.40**.

61-66   The next three couplets ironically praise the servile devotion of the poor lover. Note the ANAPHORA of *pauper*.

61-62   The poor lover will always be yours (*tibi semper*).

in tenero fixus . . . latere Note the none-too-subtle erotic double entendre.

63–64   The poor man will clear the way for Delia on the crowded streets of Rome. This was a function normally performed by the lesser members of the retinue accompanying senators through the forum.

65–66   The ultimate in self-abasement the poor man will lead Delia to visit her other lovers (*amicos*). Assume *te*.

uincla = SYNECDOCHE (part for the whole) for sandals

67–68   His pleading is in vain. Her door only opens for the hand full (*plena . . . manu*) of money.

est percutienda = pass. periphrastic

69–70   The poet's rival is warned not to take his advantage for granted. The wheel of Fortune turns for all.

timeto = fut. imperative

In the pentameter, note the interlaced word order imitating the topsy-turvy rotations of Fortune's wheel.

71–74   The physical comedy of the rival lover peering round, running away, returning as a passerby, and discreetly coughing before the door is worthy of Chaplin or the early cinematic greats.

71–72   The key question in this couplet is who is *quidam*: Tibullus or yet another rival? From Fortune's perspective it's all the same.

Note the contrast between *frustra* in **67** and *non frustra* here.

75–76   a final oracular warning. *Nescio quid* = "something."

utere = imperative

↶ *1.9*

Tibullus rails against his beloved, Marathus. The young man has been selling his favors to the highest bidder, a married man whose wife has a young lover of her own. Marathus will be punished for his venality by failing in his attempts to win the girl Pholoe, first mentioned in 1.8. The poem illustrates one of the truisms of elegy, the poor poet's disadvantage in relation to a wealthy rival.

This poem also demonstrates the fundamentally different way sexual identity was conceived in the ancient world. The bisexual nature of Marathus's interests are reflected in those of the poet and his wealthy rival. In effect, bisexuality in this context is a misnomer. It assumes a combination of two normally mutually exclusive forms of sexual identity: heterosexuality and homosexuality. But, as this poem makes clear, these forms of sexual identity, based on the gender of one's sexual object choice, are not operative in a Roman context. Roman morality was highly structured and rule bound, but those rules were based on premises fundamentally different from modern western norms.

Poem 1.9 continues the tale of the poet's homoerotic distress, but the situation has become considerably more complicated. Marathus's affections have been stolen by a *diues amator,* who is portrayed as a doltish and unappealing old man with an unfaithful young wife and a drunken, sluttish sister. Marathus also has his own female beloved, Pholoe, whom the poet prays will treat Marathus in the same fashion as the latter has treated him. The poem is memorable for some of the most vivid invective in all of elegy, worthy of Catullus's iambic poems or even Juvenal. The following lines show a very different Tibullus from the oft-pictured dreamy and melancholic lover:

> at te, qui puerum donis corrumpere es ausus,
>   rideat adsiduis uxor inulta dolis,
> et cum furtiuo iuuenem lassauerit usu,   55
>   tecum interposita languida ueste cubet.
> semper sint externa tuo uestigia lecto,
>   et pateat cupidis semper aperta domus;

nec lasciua soror dicatur plura bibisse
    pocula uel plures emeruisse uiros.   60
illam saepe ferunt conuiuia ducere baccho,
    dum rota Luciferi prouocet orta diem. (1.9.53–62)

[But you who dared to corrupt the boy with gifts, may
your wife mock you with impunity with her unstinting
tricks. And when she has worn out her young man
with furtive use, may she lie with you fully clothed.
And may there ever be the tracks of others in your bed,
and may your house ever be open to the lusty, and your
slutty sister not be said to have drunk more cups or
used up more men (than your wife). Often they say she
draws out the party with wine until the risen chariot of
the Morning Star calls forth the day.]

This is strong stuff. But the layers of IRONY and overdetermination
in such a poem are impossible to unravel. Who is making fun of
whom? Is Marathus being attacked for yielding to the *diues amator*?
The *diues amator* for corrupting the love of a boy who was obviously
unfaithful from the start? The female relatives of the *diues amator*
for their lack of morality? The *diues amator* for his inability to assert
his masculine control over their behavior? Or the poet for inserting
himself in such a ridiculous series of hapless events?

    As always in Tibullus there is no unimpeachable perspective from
which to make such a determination. This is, of course, part of what
makes the Tibullan dream text so endlessly fascinating. On the one
hand, its pose is that of absolute simplicity: the simple farmer, the
devoted lover, the hapless pederast. On the other, the poet's immense
literary craft has created a kind of bottomless text where each layer
of meaning dissolves into the next, like the scenes inside a dream.

1–2   Why did you swear, if you intended to deceive? The contorted
        syntax betrays the poet's emotional discomfort.

        fueras . . . laesurus literally, "had been about to harm"

miseros = transfer of epithet. It is not the "loves" but the lovers who are wretched.

foedera See on **1.5.7**.

uiolanda = fut. pass. pple.

3–4   "Sooner or later, punishment awaits oath breakers." This is the opposite of the lesson given by Priapus at **1.4.21–26**.

et si quis = "even if someone"

Poena, the Greek goddess of punishment or revenge and mother of the Furies, comes without warning (*tacitis . . . pedibus*).

5–6   A quick about face: the poet pleads that the gods let Marathus go unpunished *just this once*. Desire trumps moral principle. The basic syntax is as follows: *aequum est licere formosis numina laedere.*

impune creates an etymological pun with *Poena*.

formosis The boy's beauty is reason enough to show mercy.

7–11   "All men act through love of gain." The poet's rapid concession to the power of greed stands in contrast to the Golden Age dream of agrarian ease and innocence in **1.1**, **1.2**, **1.5**, and **2.3**, as well as his railings against the *diues amator* in **1.4**.

7–8   The farmer is no different from the soldier and the merchant in poem **1**.

urget We expect *terram* as the object, but the poet offers *durum terrae . . . opus* as an elegant variation.

9–10   The sea-roving merchant is a familiar figure for greed.

petituras modifies *rates*.

parentia < *pareo*

The contrast between the *instabiles . . . rates* and the *sidera certa* that lead them is underlined by the CHIASTIC word order.

11–12 Up to the bucolic diaeresis (break at the end of the fourth foot), this transitional couplet summarizes the previous point. It then turns to envision future punishments, if Marathus persists in his behavior.

illa modifies *munera*.

uertat = jussive subjunctive

liquidas . . . aquas See **1.5.76**.

13-14   As punishment, Marathus will be forced to accompany the *diues amator* on a long journey, which will cost him his looks. Note the shift from the subjunctive to the fut. indicative.

poenas See **4** and **5**.

puluis and **coma** both = the subject of *detrahet. Coma* = poetic sing. for pl.

15-16   Marathus will be sunburned and his tender (*inualidos*) feet worn away by the rigors of travel. Note that line 15 is all spondees, except for the fourth foot, emphasizing the slow pounding heat of the desert sun.

17-28   The poet's speech of warning is a study in passive-aggressive psychology.

17-18   Note the menacing ALLITERATIVE sibilants in the pentameter.

19-20   The shift from the subjunctive (**12**) to the fut. (**13-16**) to the pres. indicative (**18, 20**) denotes a shift from a wish to a prediction to an affirmation of reality.

captus See **11**.

uiolauit See **2** and **1.2.81**.

21-22   Before I offend against love, visit the tortures of a slave up on me. See on **1.5.5-6**. Note that he pictures the violent retribution the poet warns Marathus against as inflicted upon himself. The combination of masochistic enjoyment and sadistic intimidation is deft.

23-24   The poet addresses Marathus directly: "there is a god who forbids deceptions." The text of pentameter is controversial. I follow the reading of the oldest manuscript.

celandi = gen. sing. of the gerund. Compare **3**.

paranti modifies *tibi* and takes *peccare* as complementary infinitive.

25-26   Even if discreet, your slave, when drunk, will give you away.

lene This reading is not universally accepted. If correct, the neuter is used adverbially with the idea that the god "gently" loosens the servant's tongue with wine. *Leue* is another common manuscript reading. Both are relatively rare as adverbs, *leniter* and *leuiter* being more common. The sixteenth-century humanist, Muretus, proposed *saepe*, which is tempting.

27-28   If your servants don't give you away, you'll talk in your sleep.

somno domitos = "those tamed by sleep," a vivid image. *Domitos* is substantive.

29-30   **haec ego dicebam** See **1.5.35**, *haec mihi fingebam*, both passages indicate a moment of bravado or optimism followed by acknowledged abjection.

fleuisse . . . **procubuisse** = pf. infinitives

pudet the shame of being a supplicant

31-32   Marathus swore more than once (*iurabas*) that his love was not for sale (*uendere*).

nullo . . . pondere . . . gemmis = ablatives of price

fidem a foundational Roman value of trusted relations between equal actors. A *foedus* (**2**) was founded on *fides*.

33-34   Campania in central Italy was proverbial for its fertility, and the Falernian region in its north produced among the finest Roman wines.

Bacchi cura the object of the god's concern, in apposition to *Falernus ager*

35-36   The boy was so convincing, or the poet so desirous, that his words could snatch away the belief that the stars shine in the sky.

illis . . . uerbis = abl. of means

eriperes = potential subjunctive in the past

The construction is *eriperes . . . mihi sidera . . . lucere*. This use of an object clause with *eripio* is quite rare. Perrelli (2002) has the most complete list of parallels. As he observes, the whole couplet is a kind of "antiadunaton," or a reversal of the standard figure of impossibility ("adunaton"). *puras fluminis esse uias* is coordinate with *sidera lucere*. The text here is contested, but I have printed the consensus reading of the codices. *Puras* in this context means, "clear, flowing."

37-38 A still naïve Tibullus (*non ego fallere doctus*) was taken in by Marathus's false tears.

quin etiam = "but indeed"

39-40 "What was I to do [but dry your tears], except that you were also in love with a girl." The transition is not particularly logical, but marks a pivot to Marathus's relation with Pholoe as opposed to simply with Tibullus and the *diues amator*. This pivot allows for parallels to be developed between the poet's situation and that of Marathus.

faciam = deliberative subjunctive

fores = *esses*

The text of the pentameter is disputed, with most of the codices having *sed* in place of *sit* in one of the two places it is printed here, but there is no consensus among the manuscripts on which *sit* should be replaced by *sed*. Plus a few codices have the present text. The correction of *sit* to *sed* is colorless and obvious, and for that reason to be suspected, especially given the confusion about which *sit* is to be replaced. By contrast, as Putnam (1973) notes, "the repetition of *sit* helps the litany of the curse."

41-42 True to the principles enunciated by Priapus in **1.4**, the poet served as the boy's servile accomplice in his assignations with Pholoe. Compare the praise of the poor lover in **1.2.65**.

uerbis ... conscius i.e., aware of the words exchanged between Marathus and his *puella*

multa ... nocte = "late at night"

43-44 The poet served as go-between.

saepe insperanti uenit tibi compare Catullus 107.1-2, *si quicquam cupido optantique optigit umquam/ insperanti* and 107.5-6 *restituis cupido atque insperanti, ipsa refers te/ nobis.*

munere nostro = "by our offices"

adoperta = "covered up, veiled," to prevent recognition by others

latuit clausas . . . fores Smith (1913) still has the most convincing explanation, "Marathus goes to her house and the girl, who has already stolen her way (*uenit*) to the door and is waiting for him inside, lets him in."

45–46   "Then I was I done in."

interii Fantasies of death are common in elegy. *Morior* and *pereo* are more commonly used.

confisus < *confido*

poteram = "I could have been"

cautior = compar. pple. < *caueo*

47–48   **quin etiam** = "but indeed"

attonita = literally "thunderstuck," both "inspired" and "crazy"

laudes . . . canebam = "I was singing songs of praise," i.e., composing poetic panegyrics

nostri possibly poetic pl., but probably including Marathus as well

nostri Pieridumque = gen. with verb of emotion (Gildersleeve and Lodge ¶ 377)

49–50   Let Vulcan burn those songs in rapid flame (*rapida . . . flamma*) and let a river wash them away! Compare Catullus 70.4, *in uento et rapida scribere oportet aqua.*

uelim = potential subjunctive

torreat and **deleat** The omission of *ut* is common in poetry.

51–52   Be gone since your beauty is for sale!

absis = jussive subjunctive

plena . . . manu See **1.5.67–68.**

53–74   The focus shifts from the venal boy to his corruptor. Compare **1.5.69–76.**

53–54 Note the casual assumption not only that the *diues amator* has an *uxor* but also that he expects her to be monogamous. For more on this and the following couplets, see the introduction to the commentary on this poem.

te . . . rideat "may she laugh at, mock you"

55–56 The wife wearing out a young man with constant "use" recalls the vivid imagery found in Catullus (e.g., final stanza of poem 11), whose work offers a number of important intertexts for this poem. The commentators remind us that *usus* stands for *usus Veneris*, but the idea of the wife reducing the young man to a tool for her pleasure is not far away.

lassauerit Note the shift from subjunctive to fut. pf.

languida = "sexually spent"

57–58 May your house and bed be open to all comers!

sint . . . pateat jussive subjunctive

uestigia = a vivid if ultimately grotesque image

59–60 And we already know about your sister!

plura . . . plures Understand *quam tua uxor*, compounding the insult.

emeruisse "the verb usually refers to serving out one's time in the army, and its use with *uiros* here may suggest the sister has worked her way through an army of men" (Maltby 2002).

61–62 Her drinking has been the talk of the town.

ferunt = "they say"

ducere = "to draw out"

baccho abl. of means

prouocet subjunctive with *dum*

rota Luciferi = the chariot of the morning star. The contrast between the refined poetic image and the scene described is to be savored.

63–64 No woman is better able to finish off a night than she!

illa = abl. of comparison

consumere with love, drinking, or both?

operum = *Veneris*

65-66   You don't even notice that your wife has learned your sister's art.

tua Understand *uxor*. But the possibility of a momentary confusion with the *soror* implies incest as well.

stultissime = vocative superl. < *stultus*

67-68   Do you think she is primping for you?

denso . . . dente = "fine tooth"

69-70   Are you really that attractive?

ista . . . facies = "that face of yours"

haec = n. pl. referring to the previous couplet

persuadet would normally take *ut* with the subjunctive.

auroque lacertos/ uinciat a very grand way of saying "she should wear golden bracelets"

Tyrio Tyrian purple was particularly expensive; see **1.2.77**.

71-72   For the sake of her young man (compare **55**), she would curse your house and fortune.

deuoueat potential subjunctive

73-74   She doesn't do this from vice, but because you are repulsive

uitio and **podagra** = abl. of cause

amplexus = acc. pl.

culta puella the elegiac ideal

75-76   Yet our boy slept with him: a truly unnatural act.

huic The shift from the second person to the demonstrative pron. displays contempt.

hunc refers to the boy.

uenerem iungere = "to mate with"

77-78   The poet claims ownership of the boy's kisses and love talk. In a context in which the poet rails against the sale of love, the claim to a proprietary interest is particularly IRONIC.

79–80   There's more than one fish in the sea!

geret . . . regna = "hold sway." Observe the POLYPTOTON (deliberate variation of forms) with *regno*.

81–82   But I will dedicate a golden palm to Venus on behalf of the penalty you will pay.

poena recalls the theme that opened the poem.

Venerique merenti *Bene merenti* is common in dedicatory inscriptions.

fixa = to the temple wall

iuuet and **notet** = jussive subjunctive

aurea palma The IRONY of a golden palm as a symbol of the poet's victory over the beloved who would sell his favors for *aurum* (**17, 18, 31, 69**) is not to be missed, especially given that victory here signifies a fantasized separation when the poet will become bound (*uinctum*) to another. Hence the *aurea palma* also marks his victory and his conquest by the new boy.

83–84   A votive inscription left by one saved from danger.

hanc = the *aurea palma*

resolutus = the opposite of *uinctum*

grata sis . . . mente = "be well disposed"

∾ 2.1

Poem 2.1 serves as an introduction to the second book and depicts for us almost a world of traditional rural piety. The occasion of the poem is the private Ambarvalia, a purification rite in which a landowner, followed by a procession of dependents—slaves, freedmen, tenant farmers—would lead the sacrifice around the borders of the estate. Prayer, sacrifice, and good cheer would then ensue. Neither Delia nor Marathus make an appearance in this poem and the first third is largely given over to a description of the rite. That section concludes with a ritual toast offered to Messalla, who in his capacity as a member of the Arval Brethren, would have been in Rome celebrating the urban version of the ritual. The toast is tasteful and

Fig. 2 Sacral-idyllic landscape paintings are frequently compared to Tibullus's soft-focus evocations of the Roman countryside. First century BC wall painting. Villa of Agrippa Postumus at Boscotrecase. Museo Archeologico Nazionale, Naples. Wikimedia Commons.

restrained. Messalla in his quasi-divine status as *trimphator* over the Aquitani is called upon to serve as the poet's Muse as he offers a hymn of praise to the country and the country gods. There follows a genealogy of civilization from the advent of agriculture to the birth of poetry. It is only, at this point, with the introduction of the role of Cupid in insuring agricultural fertility, that the poet's previous identity as the unhappy lover of Book 1 first becomes visible:

> ipse quoque inter agros interque armenta Cupido
>   natus et indomitas dicitur inter equas.
> illic indocto primum se exercuit arcu:
>   ei mihi, quam doctas nunc habet ille manus!   70
> nec pecudes, uelut ante, petit: fixisse puellas
>   gestit et audaces perdomuisse uiros. (2.1.67–72)

With four simple words the poet pulls us back into the artistically and emotionally complex world of Book 1. The most obvious are *ei mihi* "alas poor me." In a poem in which there is not a single first-person verb, this is the sole acknowledgement of the poet's subjective relation to the phenomena described. To the reader coming from Book 1, with the poems concerning Delia and Marathus fresh in mind, the cue to recast the story of the traditional rural idyll described in the poem's previous sixty-six lines as analogous to the dream of rural ease described in the first fifty-two lines of 1.1, with its accompanying urban erotic drama, could not be clearer. At the same time, this one brief exclamation is surrounded by the antonyms *indoctus* and *doctus*: where Cupid's bow was "untutored," it is now "well-practiced." These words, however, are terms of art in Alexandrian poetics. *Doctus* is the epithet applied to a master of his craft, the learned poet whose technique is flawless and who is immersed in the poetry and mythology of previous eras. Thus Tibullus becomes transformed into the master poet of love from Book 1 as Cupid comes to master his bow, and the poet's anguished cry of pain, *ei mihi*, is precisely the sign of his and Cupid's triumph.

One of Tibullus's great themes is the nostalgia for a return to a golden age of rural ease. This is not *the* Golden Age proper, which, as Tibullus makes clear in 2.3, was a period before agriculture when humans lived in absolute simplicity and harmony with the natural world. Nonetheless, the frequent theme of a kind of rural idyll joined with recollections of the Golden Age as a period before commerce, sea travel, and property, is one of the basic features of the Tibullan dream text. The logical incompatibility of these different aspects of the dream—farm life joined with pre-agricultural life—indicates that we are dealing more with poetic evocations of fundamental desires than actual propositions. Tibullus neither wants to be an actual, hands-on farmer nor to live on acorns and do without a house, property, and even clothes.

Another common theme throughout the corpus is the power and generosity of Tibullus's patron, Messalla. The current poem, introducing the second book, marries the patronage and Golden Age themes by joining the celebration of a traditional rural holiday, generally identified as the private Ambarvalia, a rite of purification, with praise of the absent Messalla. Regular daily labor is suspended in the dreamlike space of the ritual, and a harmonious world of social recognition, erotic desire, and natural plenty is evoked. Elegiac love is only mentioned at the poem's end, and the poet's new mistress, the ill-omened Nemesis, does not appear at all. The poem recalls the central passage of **1.5** in which the poet imagines Delia serving the fruits of their estate to Messalla, shortly before admitting the whole scene to be a fiction (*haec mihi fingebam*).

Poem 2.1 begins with an invocation of the gods and a call for holy silence. There is then a procession to the altar, prayer to the gods, celebratory drinking, and a toast offered to Messalla. The poem concludes with a long prayer in which is recounted the role of the country gods in the development of civilization and the evolution of poetry. The poem begins in the morning and ends in the evening, thus recounting the whole day's celebration. The final evocation of *Somnia nigra*, "nightmares," prepares us for the darker poems to come in Book 2.

1-2   Maintain holy silence as we purify the crops and fields in the ancestral manner.

   faueat Understand *linguae*, a traditional formula for maintaining ritual silence, lest anything ill-omened be uttered. Jussive subjunctive.

   lustramus generally thought to be an allusion to the festival Cato refers to as the *lustratio agri* (*Agr.* 141), in which the sacrifice is led round the lands to be purified. See also **1.1.21**. Note the pres. indicative: the ceremony is happening now, right before our eyes.

3-4   Let Bacchus and Ceres be present! Note the necessity of a balance between male and female deities, establishing the ideal of harmonious productivity.

   cornibus Bacchus is frequently portrayed with bull's horns symbolizing strength and fertility. Grapes are the natural offering to decorate them. Compare **1.5.27** and **2.3.63**.

spicis On crowns made from ears of grain for Ceres, see **1.1.15–16, 1.5.28**.

5–6   The holiday was a day of rest.

luce sacra = holy day

requiescat = jussive subjunctive

7–8   Even the oxen enjoy a respite. Since they were sacred to Ceres, they too wore crowns.

9–10   All work today is for the god.

sint operata . . . audeat = jussive subjunctive

pensis = the amount of wool weighed out for a woman to spin on a given day. In traditional life, the woman was to spin and the man was to plough.

11–12 Ritual celibacy was a common part of many rituals.

uos . . . discedat To explain the inconsistency in person and number, assume *cuicui* for *cui*.

13–14 The root meaning of *casta* is "purged," "purified." It often has a sexual meaning and, coming immediately after the invocation of ritual celibacy, this idea dominates initially, but the word takes on a broader sense of ritual cleanliness as the couplet unfolds. The n. pl. is the first evidence that the meaning might transcend the purely sexual.

manibus puris sumite fontis aquam The reference is both to the ritual washing of hands and to the sprinkling of water during the sacrifice with hands that have been washed. *Puris* thus does double duty.

15–16 Behold the consecrated lamb (*sacer agnus*) makes its way to the gleaming altars.

fulgentes . . . aras presumably because of the fire, but perhaps an altar of polished stone

uinctaque . . . olea . . . comas The priests and other members of the procession wore crowns of olive leaves.

candida = dressed in white

17–24 A prayer to the ancestral gods.

17–18 **di patrii** = native/ancestral gods, gods of our fathers. In addition to the Olympians explicitly mentioned in the poem, Bacchus and Ceres, this would include the Lares in their function as boundary gods. See **1.1.19–20**. *Di* is a frequent form of the nom. pl. in verse.

agrestes = substantive

19–20 **neu seges eludat messem fallacibus herbis** The *seges* is the mature crop of grain. It would escape the harvest in the manner of a gladiator parrying a thrust (*eludat*), either through an initial deceptive (*fallacibus*) luxuriance, when the still green shoots (*herbis*) arose, or through the presence of cheating weeds (*fallacibus herbis*). Parallels are cited by Murgatroyd (1994) for both senses.

eludat . . . timeat = jussive subjunctives

21–22 **tunc** points to the results of the prayers being fulfilled.

nitidus = both "shining" with good health and "aglow" with the warming fire

23–24 The *rusticus*, presumably a tenant of the poet or of the ritual officiant, is surrounded by the crowd of his house-born slaves (*turba uernarum*), the signs of a prosperous (*saturi*) farmer.

ante – before the fire

casas = temporary shelters for a festival

25–26 The omens are favorable.

euentura precor = "I pray things will turn out."

uiden = "do you see?" "-*Ne* sometimes cuts off a preceding -*s* . . . and often drops its own *e*" (Gildersleeve and Lodge ¶ 455).

felicibus extis = abl. of means

27–36 A toast offered to Messalla. This passage has a distinctly Horatian feel.

27–28 Bring out the fine aged vintages.

fumosos . . . Falernos Falernian wines were aged in casks stored in upper rooms where the smoke from the hearth rose to aid the maturation of the wine.

ueteris ... consulis The Roman calendar marked years by the names of the consuls. An "old consul" would indicate a well-aged wine.

Chio Chian was a light Greek wine, which was sometimes mixed with the heavier Falernian.

uincla here = "seals"

29–30   On a feast day, it's a shame not to get drunk and stumble.

celebrent jussive subjunctive. Note the PERSONIFICATION of the *uina*.

madere = "to drip," hence "to be soaked"

rubor = "to blush," and hence a cause of shame. Red, of course, is also the color of wine.

31–32   But first, let us each raise a glass to the absent Messalla.

bene Messallam Understand *ualere iubeo* or something similar.

ad pocula = "at wine," "at his cups," as opposed to "to their cups," which would take the dat.

singula uerba = "each word"

33–34   This couplet is an extended noun phrase defining the glory of Messalla.

celeber = *clarus*, "renowned," perhaps the first such usage

gentis Aquitanae ... triumphis Messalla celebrated his triumph over the Aquitanians in 27 BCE. Tibullus commemorates the triumph in poem 1.7.

uictor = "as victor," in apposition to *gloria*

intonsis ... auis = "longhaired" and hence "ancient"

35–36   The great man is summoned to serve as the poet's inspiration. His semi-divine status as *triumphator*, the momentary embodiment of Jupiter, gives him a status analogous to that of Muses.

huc ades = a regular formula at the beginning of a hymn. The god is before us.

37-66   The song of thanks to the country gods announced in the pre-
        vious couplet.

37-38   I sing the rural gods and the beginning of farming.

        uita = subject of *desueuit*. The first step in civilization is ag-
        riculture. The *querna . . . glande* symbolizes primitive pre-
        agrarian life when humans lived off the spontaneous fruits
        of the land. Acorn eating is often a sign of both primitivism
        and vanished virtue in Roman discourse. See **2.3.69** and the
        opening lines of Juvenal 6.

39-40   The rural gods first taught us to build primitive houses.

        compositis . . . tigillis = abl. absolute. Note the use of the di-
        minutive of *tignum*, "beam."

        docuere =3rd pl. pf.

41-42   **tauros . . . docuisse . . . seruitium** tamed oxen for the yoke

        plaustro supposuisse rotam "The *seruitium* of the bulls is
        transferred to the wheel through the word *supposuisse*, one
        of the regular verbs in Latin for submission to a yoke or pole"
        (Putnam 1973).

43-44   Then fruit trees were sown and gardens irrigated.

        uictus = the noun modified by *feri*, not the pple.

45-46   Then wine was made. This occurred in the fall. The next
        three couplets continue to review the agricultural calendar,
        but in reverse. Moving from fall to summer to spring to
        winter.

        dedit = "yielded"

        securo = act., "that takes away care." *Sobria* also = act., "that
        keeps sober." The mixture of wine with water is a sign of mod-
        erate, civilized behavior.

47-48   Then harvests come in summer's heat.

        sideris is generally thought to be the sun, since the grain har-
        vest happened before the rising of the Dog Star.

        cum introducing a temporal clause

        aestu = abl. of description

flauas . . . comas = the stalks of ripe grain

annua = "every year"

49–50   In spring, the bee brings flowers to the hive to fill its combs with honey. The syntax and prosody of this couplet is rather complex.

leuis could go with either *flores* or *apis.*

uerno could go with either *rure* or *alueo. Alueo* is pronounced and scanned like *aluo* through a figure known as SYNIZESIS (Gildersleeve and Lodge ⁋ 727).

flores Aristotle thought bees actually constructed their hives out of flowers. In terms of honey production, *flores* may stand METONYMICALLY for the nectar. See the discussion in Murgatroyd (1994) and Maltby (2002).

51–52   The ancient ploughman was the first poet.

satiatus < *satio* (1), i.e. when he has "had enough" of the plough, but note the pun also on *satio -onis*, "sowing."

certo . . . pede The rustic farmer's crude songs were beaten out in a sure-footed rhythm that would later become the unfailing meter (*certo pede*) of the modern poet.

53–54   Then, "full" (*satur*) of food and drink, he would play a song on an oaten reed. The line is very reminiscent of Vergil, *Eclogues* 1.2 and 10.51. Note the punning relation between *satiatus/satio* and *satur.*

arenti pres. pple. < *areo*

ornatos . . . deos statues decorated for a holiday. Compare **1.1.13–16**.

diceret = "recite, sing"

55–56   We move from *rustica uerba*, to accompanied song, to full, if primitive, choruses and theatrical performances.

minio . . . rubenti The reference here is not clear. It may refer to a kind or primitive mask for dramatic performance made by painting the face. It may refer to the use of red paint to decorate gods of fertility and thus presumably their worshipers.

Or it may simply refer to celebratory face painting such as found in carnival and sporting celebrations to this day. All of these hypotheses have been advanced in the scholarship, nor is it clear that they are mutually exclusive.

Bacche Bacchus/Dionysus was closely associated with the origins of ancient dramatic performances.

57–58 This couplet alludes to the mythic origins of tragedy, according to which it was named for the *tragos* or "goat" that was given for the best song (*ōidēi*).

hircus is the subject of *auxerat* with *dux* and *munus* in apposition. The syntax is complex and the transmission of the text not secure. Acceptance of the vulgate entails a number of metrical irregularities. The version printed here accepts several emendations, but follows the text presented by many modern editions (Smith 1913, Postgate 1915, Ponchont 1950, Putnam 1973, and, with one slight variation, Murgatroyd 1994). It yields good sense and has no metrical anomalies. For the opposing case, see Maltby (2002).

huic = Bacchus

59–60 The country is the origin of Roman piety.

pucr Children were under the care of the *Lares*. See on **17–18**.

61–62 Where for boys their fundamental obligations are religious, for girls theirs are domestic: specifically wool-working.

curam here = *negotium*, "work, activity, business"

lucida = bright, white

ouis = the subject of *gerit*

63–64 Spinning wool was the most traditional and iconic of female tasks. When Augustus wanted to demonstrate the piety of his household, he made a display of Livia and his daughter spinning wool.

Each day a certain *pensum* of wool was weighed out, which was held on a distaff (*colus*) and pulled onto a spindle (*fusus*). The latter was spun by the thumb (*apposito pollice*).

65–66 Woman poets were rare in the ancient world, with several notable exceptions (Sappho, Corinna, Sulpicia). Tibullus is unique in attributing the origin of poetry in equal measure to both genders. On the one hand, the ploughman first sang (*cantauit*) when *satiatus* from *adsiduo aratro* (**51–52**). On the other, the woman at her weaving, *adsidue* in service to Minerva, *cantat* to the beat of her loom. In both cases, song marks the moment where organized labor separates culture from nature.

Mineruae the goddess of weaving and craft

latere < *later* = a loom weight used to keep the warp tight, poetic sing. for pl.

67–68 Cupid too was born in the country. Note how the previous hexameter ends with *Minerua*, the virgin goddess in her role as patron deity of pious female labor, and this ends with *Cupido*, the natural force of desire. Ideally these forces are in balance, but the tension between them threatens to undermine that equilibrium at every turn. It is the regularity of ritual that seeks to bind the centripetal forces of culture to the centrifugal forces of desire.

indomitas . . . equas Mares were considered particularly lustful. Taming is a frequent METAPHOR for marriage in the ancient world.

69–70 **ei mihi** a glancing acknowledgment of the poet's role as an erotic elegist

doctas . . . manus Cupid's increased sophistication coincides with that of his poets. As he learns to wield his bow, learned elegy is born. *Doctus* is a word of approbation in Alexandrian and neoteric poetics.

71–72 Cupid uses his new-found skills to wound girls and tame men.

73–74 The poet rehearses standard comic scenes: the youth who wastes the family fortune on girls and the old man performing a paraclausithyron. See **1.1.71–74**.

hic = *Cupido*

limen ad iratae = *ad limen iratae*, poetic use of the postposition. *Iratae* = substantive.

pudenda = gerundive

75-76 Cupid takes over the role of Venus in **1.2.15–22**. The poet uses this passage to establish the relation between his new work in Book 2 and his earlier work in Book 1.

transgressa modifies *puella*.

custodes ... iacentes = "the sleeping guards"

tenebris = abl. of description

77-78 A wonderful description of the girl groping her way through the dark toward her young lover.

suspensa timore "the graphic and economical suspense combines 'on tenterhooks' ... and 'raised on tiptoe'" (Murgatroyd 1994).

manus = subject of *explorat*

79-80 "Wretched are those *Amor* oppresses, but happy those to whom he is gentle." The couplet is worthy of Ovid, who would later join Tibullus in the circle around Messalla.

leniter adflat like a gentle breeze on a ship

81-82 Love is invited to the feast, so long as he puts aside his capacity to wound.

sancte = vocative

dapibus festis = "for our feasts," dat. of advantage

sagittas ... faces proverbial attributes of Love or Cupid

83-84 "Call the honored god (*Amor*) openly for the herd, but silently for oneself." The poet returns to the ritual frame of the poem.

uos = the gathered celebrants

celebrem Amor shares the same attribute as Messalla (**33**).

uocate/ uoce solemn archaic language

85-86 Rather let each shout out his desires openly: for the crowd is noisy and the pipe is playing loud.

Phrygio tibia curua sono The Phrygian flute consisted of two pipes, the longer of which was curved at the end. Phrygian music was associated with orgiastic rites and thought to inspire uncontrollable desires.

87–88 **ludite** = "it's time to party." As night falls and the drinking continues, the festivities begin in earnest.

Nox iungit equos Night joins the horses to its chariot.

matris Night is the mother of the stars.

lasciuo sidera fulua choro The stars follow in a lusty chorus.

89–90 Afterwards comes Sleep and Dreams.

nigra These dreams may be nightmares. Sleep is related to death. The poem comes full circle, from the morning's affirmations of life and piety, to the evening's licentiousness and potential oblivion.

∾ 2.3

This poem in many ways is an IRONIC return to the rural idyll that forms much of the backdrop to Book 1. But this is not a world without labor, as dreamed of in poem **1.1**. It is a fallen world of struggle in which the poet pictures himself as a literal *seruus amoris*, sunburned from his labors, with blisters on his tender hands. Delia too we find out, late in the poem, has been replaced by the ominously named Nemesis. This sophisticated poem both recalls the Golden Age world posited in Book 1 and inverts it. It also contains Tibullus's longest mythological exemplum, the story of Apollo and Admetus (lines 11–32).

The basic outline is clear. The beloved has left the city and gone to the country with her new lover, a nouveau riche military man, a virtual calc of the *miles gloriosus* of the comic tradition. The poet returns to his dream of the Golden Age at the poem's end, before his final submission to the demands of the beloved. Bring on the whips! Bring on the chains! He will willingly plough the fields of his rival's estate.

Where the amorous world of Book 1 is all but missing from the opening programmatic poem of Book 2, except for the subtle signs just discussed, in 2.3 it is fully on display and yet completely inverted.

Gone now are Delia and Marathus. Enter the aptly named Nemesis. Where in Book 1, the poet composed impossible dreams of a life of ease with Delia on his modest country estate, in Book 2 he will follow Nemesis and her *diues amator* to the country, where he will become a common field slave and engage in hard labor:

> o ego, cum aspicerem dominam, quam fortiter illic   5
>   uersarem ualido pingue bidente solum
> agricolaeque modo curuum sectarer aratrum,
>   dum subigunt steriles arua serenda boues!
> nec quererer quod sol graciles exureret artus,
>   laederet et teneras pussula rupta manus. (2.3.5–10) 10

Where the Tibullus of 1.1.8 will plant fruit trees with an easy hand (*facilis manus*), the poet of 2.3 does real labor and receives real blisters. Tibullus, however, should not hesitate. Even Apollo, we are told, humbled himself for his beloved, herding cattle for the love of Admetus in an allusion to Callimachus's hymn to Apollo:

> Delos ubi nunc, Phoebe, tua est, ubi Delphica Pytho?
>   nempe Amor in parua te iubet esse casa. (2.3.27–28)

But where the Tibullus of the first book dreams of a world in which simple piety, social form, and erotic desire coincide, the Tibullus of 2.3 imagines a countryside of masochistic self-subjection:

> ducite: ad imperium dominae sulcabimus agros:
>   non ego me uinclis uerberibusque nego. (2.3.79–80)

The reign of Nemesis is one of cruelty that stands in stark and IRONIC contrast to the ideal traditional world portrayed in the Ambarvalia celebration of **2.1** and the idyllic dream of Book 1. With her entrance, the dream becomes a nightmare.

1-2   The poem opens with a clear recollection of the themes of
        Book 1. Tibullus's *puella* is in the country, and the poet would
        have to be *ferreus* not to follow her. Compare **1.2.67**. None-
        theless, there are clear differences. Rather than pleading for
        his beloved to join him in a rural idyll, the *puella* is here held
        (against her will?) in the country, and he must depart the city
        to be with her. The poet signals that the world we have come
        to expect is turned upside down.

        Cornute = a friend of Tibullus, addressed in 2.2, otherwise
        unknown

3-4   In an inversion of the *praeceptor amoris* figure, *Amor* here be-
        comes the pupil of the ploughman as *Venus* migrates from the
        soft world of the city to the harsh reality of the country.

5-6   The lover will follow his beloved not to a rural paradise but to
        a realm of real agricultural *labor*. Compare **1.1. 29–30**.

        Hiatus after *o* in exclamations is common.

        cum = "on the condition that"

        dominam = the necessary counterpart to the poet as *seruus
        amoris*

        quam = "how"

        fortiter = "strongly, bravely"; the IRONY of the soft poet pre-
        tending to show his manhood by taking up servile labor is to
        be savored.

7-8   **curuum** The plough had a curved handle.

        sectarer The frequentative shows this not to be a one-time
        sojourn.

        steriles arua serenda boues The IRONY of the CHIASTIC con-
        struction should be noted. Castrated bulls turn under fields
        to be sown, even as the emasculated poet follows in their
        wake.

9-10   The inversion of expected role continues with the eleboration
        of specific details: the poet's delicate (*graciles*) limbs are burnt
        by the sun and his hands blistered by the plough.

quererer = potential subjunctive. The entire scenario remains merely a hypothetical possibility.

pussula a rare word in poetry, designed to introduce a realistic air

11–30   The story of Apollo tending the herds of Admetus, king of Pherae in Thessaly (Callimachus, *Hymns* 2.47–54), is a rare direct display of Alexandrian learning in Tibullus. Note the ease with which the poet compares his own servile labors to win Nemesis with Apollo's to win Admetus. Apollo's were ultimately in vain and do not augur well for Tibullus.

11–12   All of Apollo's gifts—his beauty, his lyre, his unshorn locks, his skill with medicinal herbs—have proved no match for love.

pauit < *pasco*

cithara Apollo as god of the lyre is also god of poetry

profueruntue The *-ue* logically goes with *comae*.

13–14   **medicae . . . artis** partitive gen.

14a–14c   The inclusion of an aitiological myth on the origin of cheese-making is both humorous and a typically Callimachean touch.

The passage is clearly corrupt, owing to the loss of at least one pentameter, which must have included a verb such as *dicitur* or *fertur* on which the infinitives *docuisse* and *obriguisse* depend (**14b**). Apollo must be understood as the subject of the first and *lacteus liquor* of the second.

ipse emphasizes Apollo's self-abasement in performing such menial labors.

15–16   A basket of rushes is woven to strain the whey. Note the predominance of precise, almost technical vocabulary in a lowly context. The incongruity of Alexandrian learning in a rustic setting is part of the humor.

iunci = gen. of material

rara . . . uia an allusion to Apollo's admonition to the poet in Callimachus's *Aitia* (1.27–28) to avoid the common way and keep to untrodden paths

17-18   Apollo's sister, Diana, blushes in embarrassment at his *déclassé* existence.

illo . . . gestante = abl. absolute. Compare **1.1.31–32**.

erubuisse = pf. infinitive < *erubesco*

19-20   The mooing cattle often interrupted the god of poetry's song. The parallel with the poet's own unappreciated labors should be observed. Note the ANAPHORA of *quotiens*. This couplet is metrically identical with the preceding one.

Ausae goes with *boues*, an example of HYPERBATON or the artistic disruption of normal word order. Assume *sunt*. "The structure of the couplet mirrors the daring disruption of the song" (Putnam 1973).

rumpere mugitu Note the clever collocation of ASSONANCE and ONOMATOPOEIA.

21-22   Apollo was the god of prophecy, but since he had moved to the country, his oracles were unmanned.

trepidis . . . rebus may be either dat. or abl. *Trepidus* is here used in act. sense, "causing anxiety."

petiere = 3rd pl. pf. < *peto*

domum = accusative of limit of motion (Gildersleeve and Lodge ¶ 337)

23-24   Apollo's famous locks have become a source of pain to his mother as they have become coarse and bristled. Apollo's long hair was a sign of his ephebic status. In Rome, such hair was a sign of effeminacy. The poet and his god will both sacrifice the signs of their conventional identities to become slaves of love.

Note the ANAPHORA of *saepe*. Following immediately on the ANAPHORIC pair of couplets in **17–20**, this sequence asks to be taken together, offering a humorous counterpoint to the poet's plaintive tone. The images of Apollo interrupted by mooing cattle, his temples' desertion, and his mother worrying about his hair summon a smile from the reader, who must then ask how seriously are we to take the poet's situation, which the exemplum is supposed to illustrate.

Latona = the mother of Apollo and Diana by Jupiter

nouerca = Juno. In Rome, as in fairytales, stepmothers were bywords for malice.

25-26   This colorless couplet repeats the same basic idea as the previous one. One has to wonder if it is not a late scribal gloss.

aspiceret . . . quaereret potential subjunctives in past time

27-28   The poet directly addresses the god.

Delos . . . Delphica Pytho The two most important temples of Apollo were at Delos and Delphi. The poet brackets the verse with the ALLITERATIVE pair. *Pytho* was the original name of Delphi.

ubi . . . ubī The use of two different quantities for the same word in the same line is striking.

29-32   The next two couplets elaborate the classic Tibullan contrast between a past Golden Age (*olim*) and a fallen present (*nunc*). Note the emphatic ALLITERATION of *felices* and *fabula . . . fabula*.

The precise interpretation of these lines is contested and the thought is compressed. Does *felices* refer to the *aeternos . . . deos* or to an unexpressed *nos*? Both are implied. Does *fabula* mean the "subject of gossip" or a "fiction," an "idle tale"? Again, both are implied. A god doing such things in the present would be regarded as a scandal and an "idle tale," but the lover would rather be the subject of gossip than a god without love (see Murgatroyd 1994 for a review of the relevant positions).

fertur = "it is said"

puduisse = pf. infinitive < *pudet*

mauult = 3rd pres. indicative < *malo*

33-34   This couplet is difficult and most editors see its sense as incomplete and posit a lacuna after it. The gist is that Cupid with a stern face (*tristi fronte*) has ordered Tibullus's rival to set up camp in his own household (i.e., with Nemesis). *Castra*, of course, brings to mind the TROPE of *militia amoris*.

quisquis in this context is contemptuous.

is is the subject of *es* since it refers to *tu*.

35–42   This series of couplets plays a kind of fugue on the theme of *praeda* or "loot," contrasting the poet with his wealthy rival. The word is repeated four times in three couplets in ANAPHORIC repetition. *Praedator*, the agent noun, begins the fourth.

35–36   In the current Iron Age (*ferrea . . . saecula*), loot, not love, is praised.

est operata = "is engaged in"

37–38   Loot is the origin of war and the suffering it entails.

feras acies The lines of the contending armies are imaged as wild beasts.

cruor . . . caedes mors Note the progression.

propior here = "early"

39–40   Sea travel was regarded as inherently dangerous and a sign of the passing of the Golden Age. Naval warfare was thus a kind of double (*geminare*) danger.

pericula = the subject of *geminare*

bellica . . . rostra the iron plated prows of warships, acc. pl.

dubiis . . . ratibus The image is that of unreliable little rafts not proud naval vessels.

41–42   War is undertaken precisely so that men can acquire the kind of vast estates on which Tibullus's rival holds Nemesis now.

obsidere here = "to occupy," but the more common meaning, "to besiege," is clearly appropriate to the larger martial context

pascat = "to use as pasturage," an uncommon sense

oue = instrumental abl.

43–44   The competition among the Roman elite to build ever grander and more elaborate homes and estates was a recurrent topic of the literature of the period and seen to represent a moral failing. Compare Horace, *Odes* 2.15.

lapis externus = imported stone

curae Compare line 31.

tumultu = abl. of attendant circumstances

mille columna iugis The HYPERBOLE of a single column so large it takes 1,000 teams of oxen to carry it underlines the ridiculous lengths to which the rich and newly rich went in this competition.

45–46   Luxury fishponds were created for the villas of the elite by closing (*claudit*) off portions of the sea with a breakwater (*moles*). The formerly swift fish become lazy (*lentus*) and heedless (*neglegat*) of the winter storms, an image more fitting of the elite themselves than their fish.

hibernas . . . minas = the subject of *adesse*

47–48   The poet transitions back to his own simple life in a gesture reminiscent of **1.1**. Samian and Cumaean earthenware was a byword for old-fashioned simplicity.

trahant = "draw out, prolong." The simple jugs of wine draw out the joys of the banquet.

49–50   But if girls love wealth, then let the loot pour in! There is more than a little humor in how quickly the poet's moral stand collapses.

diuitibus = m. substantive

ueniant hortatory subjunctive. Note the ALLITERATIVE pattern *ueniant . . . Venus optat opes.*

51–52   The whole couplet is a purpose clause dependent on *ueniant praedae.*

luxuria Nemesis fluat The poet's beloved will be dripping with extravagance. Note that the *x* in *luxuria* is a double consonant and thus makes the first syllable long by position. Nemesis is here named for the first time.

incedat a stately gait

53–58   The poet fantasizes his beloved's progress through the city clothed in the luxuries he will provide. Note the ANAPHORIC sequence of *illa . . . illi . . . illi.*

53-54 Coan silks were known for their sheerness and their luxury.

auratas . . . uias stripes made of golden bands or thread. Compare **2.3.16**.

55-56 Let her be accompanied by slaves imported from the Far East.

sint = jussive subjunctive

Solis an *ex commune* construction with *ignis* and *equis*. The horses that pulled the chariot of the sun were a commonplace of myth.

57-58 Africa and Tyre will compete to offer her dyed fabrics of great expense. Observe the way in which the poet frames the pentameter with the two place names and then creates a CHIASTIC effect by placing *puniceum* next to *Africa*. *Puniceus* was a bright red purple dye produced in North Africa and associated with Carthage (*Punicus*). *Puniceus* was derived from *Phoeniceus,* and the Carthaginians were in origin Phoenecian. The chief Phoenecian city was Tyre, itself the home of a famous purple dye (*purpureum*). The pentameter graphically enacts this complex relation.

Tyros = nom. sing.

59-60 This is a transitional couplet taking us from the poet's fantasy of future wealth back to Nemesis's current "captivity" on the country estate of his nouveau riche rival. It is a difficult couplet and emended by some editors. Others assume a lacuna after **57–58**.

The essential problem is what are the *nota* and to whom are they known: for if we take them as referring to what comes before, this is puzzling, given the avowedly hypothetical status of the poet's dreamed-of new riches. If we take them as referring to what comes after, the transition is unduly harsh, especially for Tibullus, who favors the all but seamless transition. The emendation of *nota* to *uota* ("wished for things") is tempting, especially given the very small nature of the change (see Murgatroyd 1994). The manuscript tradition, however, is unanimous in reporting *nota*, although even that is not conclusive. It may simply mean the corruption happened early.

regnum . . . tenet = "to have complete control"

gypsatos . . . pedes Slaves for auction had their feet marked white with gypsum.

61-62 This couplet too is filled with controversy and no one of the major manuscripts yields a completely satisfactory reading. The version printed here is that found in Smith (1913), Ponchont (1950), Putnam (1973), and with one variant, that of Lenz (1936) and Lenz and Galinsky (1972). It yields good sense and involves accepting no words not found in the tradition.

The poet directly addresses his rival with a formula often found in curses, *at tibi*. He asks the field (*dura seges*) to pay off the debt (*persoluat*) owed the seeds (*semina*) entrusted to it with no good faith (*nulla . . . fide*). The language is a curious mix of the agricultural and the financial, perhaps appropriate to the world of a nouveau riche farming magnate.

The antecedent of *qui* = *tibi*.

63-64 The poet continues his curse and calls directly upon Bacchus.

tener because the god is a youth

65-66 Beautiful girls cannot be dragged off to the country with impunity! The IRONY, of course, is that this is precisely Tibullus's fantasy in Book 1.

non tanti sunt tua musta even Bacchus, respectfully here addressed as *pater*, must recognize that the new wine he is charged with protecting is not of such great value as to let the rival get away with such a crime. *Tanti* = gen. of value.

67-76 If these are the consequences of civilization, then let us return to the simplicity of the Golden Age.

67-68 Organized agriculture is a sign of the fall from the Golden Age, when the earth spontaneously yielded its bounty.

ualeant fruges = "farewell to crops!"

modo + subjunctive in a conditional wish = "provided only"

alat and **bibantur** jussive subjunctives

69-70   The image of acorn-chomping primitives making love in the
        open air is worthy of the satirists.

        habuisse = pf. infinitive < *habeo*

71-72   Note how the word order of the pentameter builds an image of
        amorous joys enjoyed in the heart of a shady valley, the pasto-
        ral *locus amoenus*.

        gaudia is frequently a sexual euphemism.

73-74   In the Golden Age there were neither doors nor guards, and
        consequently no *exclusi amatores*.

        exclusura < *excludo*

        ianua Compare **1.2.7–10**.

        mos . . . ille = vocative with *redi* as imperative. A vivid
        formulation.

75-76   We have lost the hexameter. The subject seems to be once
        again the happiness of the past, though the comic factor is not
        to be discounted. The image of Rome's elite willingly trading
        their luxury goods for animal skins to cover equally shaggy
        bodies was designed to provoke hilarity.

        tegant = jussive subjunctive

77-78   Back to the fallen present. Luxury cannot compensate for the
        loss of the beloved.

        mea Understand *puella*.

        copia = "opportunity"

        laxam = "flowing," a sign of luxury

79-80   But we will submit to the rule of our mistress.

        ducite = "Haul me off."

Glossary and Index of Technical Terms

~ references are to page numbers in this volume ~

ONOMATOPOEIA use of words that sound like the subject described, 49, 100

OXYMORON a noun with a contradictory modifier, such as "a loquacious silence," 45, 47, 59

PARANOMASIA a play on similar words, like *me* and *mea*, 31

PARATACTIC CONSTRUCTION the use of juxtaposition rather than subordination, 44

PERSONIFICATION treating an abstraction as if it were a person, "Justice strode the earth," 38, 90

POLYPTOTON the deliberate juxtaposition of different cases of the same word, 44, 50, 84

SIMILE an explicit comparison between two terms, as in "Achilles is like a lion," 68

SYNECDOCHE part for the whole, 33, 45, 59, 61, 74

SYNIZESIS the pronunciation of two vowels as one, 92

TROPE a rhetorical figure, 37, 101

Complete Vocabulary

ā, *exclamation*, ah!

ā, **ab**, *prep.* + *abl.*, by, from

abdō, -ere, -didī -ditum, to put away, hide

abdūcō, -ere, -duxī -ductum, to lead away

absens, -entis, *adj.*, absent

abstineō, -ēre, -tinuī, -tentum, to keep away from

absum, -esse, āfuī, āfūturus, to be away

ac, *conj.*, and, also

accubō (1), to lie beside

acerbus, -a, -um, *adj.*, bitter

aceruus, -ī, *m.*, heap, pile

aciēs, -ēī, *f.*, a sharpness or edge; the battle line of an army

ad, *prep.* + *acc*, to, at; *of accompaniment*, to, by

addō, -ere, addidī, additum, to bring, add

adeō, -īre, -iī, -itum, to go to, to approach

adferō, -ferre, attulī, adlātum, to bring to

adfirmō (1), strengthen, to affirm

adflō (1), to blow on

adiungō, -ere, -iunxī, -iunctum, to join to, attach

adiuuō, -āre, -iūuī, -iūtum, help, aid

Admētus, -ī, *m.*, Admetus

admīror, -ārī, -ātus sum, to wonder at

admittō, -ere, -mīsī, -missum, to let in, take up

admoneō, -ēre, -uī, -itum, to admonish, remind

admoueō, -ēre, -mōuī, -mōtum, to move to, apply

adoperiō, -īre, -operuī, -opertum, to cover

adpōnō, -ere, -posuī, -positum, to place on

adsiduē, *adv.*, constantly

adsiduus, -a, -um, *adj.*, constant

adsuescō, -ere, -suēuī, -suētum, to become accustomed to

adsum, -esse, -fuī, -futūrus, to be present

aequus, -a, -um, *adj.*, right, fair, even

aestiuus, -a, -um, *adj.*, summer

aestus, -ūs, *m.*, boiling, heat

aetās, -ātis, *f.*, age

aeternus, -a, -um, *adj.*, eternal

Āfrica, -ae, *f.*, Africa

ager, agrī, *m.*, field

agmen, -inis, *n.*, an army on the march, a column

agna, -ae, *f.*, a lamb

agnus, -ī, *m.*, a lamb

agō, -ere, ēgī, actum, to drive; to do; to act

agrestis, -e, *adj.*, country, rustic

agricola, -ae, *f.*, farmer

āla, -ae, *f.*, wing

aliquis, aliquid, *pron.*, someone, something

alius, -a, -ud, *adj.*, other, another

alō, -ere, aluī, altum, to nourish

alter, -tera, -terum, *adj.*, one of two, the other

altus, -a, -um, *adj.* tall, deep

alueus, -ī, *m.*, a hollow cavity, a beehive

amātor, -ōris, *m.*, lover

amnis, -is, *m.*, river

amō (1), to love, make love

amor, amōris, *m.*, love

amplexus, -ūs, *m.*, encircling, embrace

ancilla, -ae, *f.*, maid

angustus, -a, -um, *adj.*, narrow

anima, -ae, *f.*, breath, soul

annus, -ī, *m.*, year

annuus, -a, -um, *adj.*, yearly, annual

ante, *adv. and prep. + acc.*, before

antiquus, -a, -um, *adj.*, ancient

anus, -ūs, *f.*, an old woman

anxius, -a, -um, *adj.*, pressed tightly, anxious, uneasy

aperiō, -īre, aperuī, apertum, to uncover, open

apertē, *adv.*, openly

apis, -is, *f.*, bee

aprīcus, -a, -um, *adj.*, open, sunny

aptus, -a, -um, *adj.*, fitted with, suitable, appropriate

aqua, -ae, *f.*, water

Aquītānus, -a, -um, *adj.*, Aquitanian

āra, -ae, *f.*, altar

arātor, -ōris, *m.*, ploughman

arātrum, -trī, *n.*, plough

arbor, -oris, *f.*, tree

arcus, -ī, *m.*, bow

ardeō, -ēre, arsī, arsum, to burn; to be passionate

ārea, -ae, *f.*, threshing-floor

āreō, -ēre, -uī, -itum, to be dry, thirsty

argentum, -ī, *n.*, silver, money

arma, -ōrum, *n. pl.*, arms

Armenius, -a, -um, *adj.*, Armenian

armentum, -ī, *n.*, cattle

armō (1), to arm

ars, artis, *f.*, art, skill

artus, -a, -um, *adj.*, close, tight

artus, -ūs, *m.*, limb

aruum, -ī, *n.*, cultivated fields, plough lands

asper, -era, -erum, *adj.*, harsh, rough, bitter

aspergō, -ere, aspersī, aspersum, to sprinkle

aspiciō, -ere, aspexī, aspectum, to look upon

aspīrō (1), to breathe upon; to inspire

at, *conj.*, but

atque, *conj.*, and, and also

atterō, -ere, -trīuī, -trītum, to rub against, to wear away

attonitus, -a, -um, *adj.*, struck by thunder, senseless, inspired

audācia, -ae, *f.*, boldness

audax, -ācis, *adj.*, bold

audeō, -ēre, ausus sum, to dare

auēna, -ae, *f.*, oats, a straw; a shepherd's oaten pipe

augeō, -ēre, auxī, auctum, to make grow, increase

auis, -is, *f.*, bird

aurātus, -a, -um, *adj.*, golden, gilded

aureus, -a, -um, *adj.*, golden

aurum, -ī, *n.*, gold

aut, *conj.*, or

auus, -ī, *m.*, grandfather

bacchus, -ī, *m.*, wine; **Bacchus**, god of wine

barba, -ae, *f.*, beard

barbarus, -a, -um, *adj.*, foreign, savage

bellicus, -a, -um, *adj.*, related to war

bellus, -a, -um, *adj.*, beautiful

bellō (1), to make war

bene, *adv.*, well

bibō, -ere, -ī, -itum, to drink

bidens, -dentis, *m.*, mattock, two-pronged hoe

blanditia, -ae, *f.*, flattery, sweet nothings

blandus, -a, -um, *adj.*, pleasing, flattering, seductive

bōs, bouis, *m./f.*, ox, cow

brūma, -ae, *f.*, wintry cold

cadō, -ere, cecidī, casum, to fall

cadus, -ī, *m.*, a large jar for wine or oil

caecus, -a, -um, *adj.*, blind

caedēs, -is, *f.*, a cutting down, blood

caedō, -ere, cecīdī, caesum, to cut, kill

caelestis, -e, *adj.*, belonging to heaven

caelum, -ī, *n.*, heaven

caeruleus (also **caerulus**), **-a, -um**, *adj.*, the color of the sky, blue

caleō, -ēre, -uī, to be warm

calidus, -a, -um, *adj.*, hot

callidus, -a, -um, *adj.*, clever, sly

Campānius, -a, -um, *adj.*, Campanian

campus, -ī, *m.*, field

canis, -is, *m.*, dog; **Canis**, the Dog Star

candidus, -a, -um, *adj.*, white, shining, gleaming

canō, -ere, cecinī, cantum, to sing

cantus, -ūs, *m.*, song, incantation

cānus, -a, -um, *adj.*, whitish-grey, grey

capella, -ae, *f.*, she-goat

capiō, -ere, cēpī, captum, to take, seize

capillus, -ī, *m.*, hair

caput, capitis, *n.*, head, person

carcer, -eris, *m.*, jail, cell

cardō, cardinis, *f.*, hinge

careō, -ēre, -uī, -itūrus, to lack

cārus, -a, -um, *adj.*, dear, expensive

carmen, -inis, *n.*, charm; song, poem

casa, -ae, *f.*, shack, hut

castrum, -ī, *n.*, military camp

castus, -a, -um, *adj.*, clean, pure, spotless

cāsus, -ūs, *m.*, fall, misfortune

catasta, -ae, *f.*, a platform on which slaves were exposed in the market

caterua, -ae, *f.*, troop, crowd

caueō, -ēre, cāuī, cautum, to beware, be cautious

causa, -ae, *f.*, cause, case

cēdō, -ere, cessī, cessum, to go; to yield, submit

celeber, -bris, -bre, *adj.*, crowded, well-attended, famous

celebrō (1), to visit frequently; to honor

celer, celeris, celere, *adj.*, swift

cēlō (1), to hide

cernō, -ere, crēuī, crētum, to distinguish, to perceive

certē, *adv.*, surely, certainly

certō (1), to struggle, compete

certus, -a, -um, *adj.*, sure

cessō (1), to give over, leave off

cēterus, -a, -um, *adj.*, other, remaining

Chīus, -a, -um, *adj.*, from the island of Chios; *often as substantive*, Chian wine

chorus, -ī, *m.*, chorus

Cilix, -icis, *adj.*, Cilician

cingō, -ere, cinxī, cinctum, to surround; to gird

cinis, -eris, *m.*, ashes

circum, *prep.* + *acc.*, around

circumdō, -dare, -dedī, -datum, to surround

cithara, -ae, *f.*, lyre

cito, *adv.*, quickly

clam, *adv.*, secretly

clamō (1), to shout aloud

classicum, -ī, *n.*, trumpet

claudō, -ere, clausī, clausum, to close

coāgula, -ae, *f.*, rennet

cōgō, -ere, coēgī, coactum, to drive, compel

collis, -is, *m.*, hill

collum, -ī, *n.*, neck

colōnus, -ī, *m.*, farmer, tenant farmer, inhabitant

color, -is, *m.*, color

columna, -ae, *f.*, column

colus, -ūs, *f.*, distaff

coma, -ae, *f.*, hair

comes, -itis, *m./f.*, traveling companion, attendant

compescō, -ere, -pescuī, -pescitum, to curb, restrain

compleō, -ēre, -plēuī, -plētum, to fill up

compōnō, -ere, -posuī, -positum, to compose, arrange, settle

concīdō, -ere, -cīdī, -cīsum, to cut up, cut down

condō, -ere, -didī, -dītum, to put together; to found; to put away

conferō, -ferre, -tulī, collātum, to put together, collect, contribute

confīdō, -ere, -fīsus sum, to have complete trust in

congerō, -ere, -gessī, -gestum, to pile up

coniunx, -iugis, *m./f.*, spouse

conscius, -a, -um, *adj.*, privy to, aware

conserō, -ere, -sēuī, -situm, to sow

consitor, -ōris, *m.*, sower

conspiciō, -ere, -spexī, -spectum, to catch sight of, behold

consuescō, -ere, -suēuī, -suētum, to accustom; to accustom oneself

consul, -is, *m.*, consul

consultō (1), to ask advice of

consūmō, -ere, -sumpsī, -sumptum, to spend, consume

contentus, -a, -um, *adj.*, satisfied

contexō, -ere, -texuī, -textum, to weave together; to fabricate by joining

contineō, -ēre, -tinuī, -tentum, to hold together, embrace

contingō, -ere, -tigī, -tactum, to touch, concern, happen

conuīuium, -ī, *n.*, banquet, dinner party

conuocō (1), to call together

cōpia, -ae, *f.*, abundance, means, opportunity

cōram, *adv.*, openly

cornū, -ūs, *n.*, horn

Cornūtus, -ī, *m.*, Cornutus

corōna, -ae, *f.*, wreath, crown

corōnō (1), to wreathe, crown

corpus, corporis, *n.*, body

corrumpō, -ere, -rūpī, -ruptum, to destroy, to break, to corrupt

Cōus, -a, -um, *adj.*, Coan, from the island of Cos

crēber, -bra, -brum, *adj.*, thick, crowded, repeated, frequent

crēdō, -ere, credidī, creditum, to entrust, trust, believe

credulus, -a, -um, *adj.*, trusting

crīnis, -is, *m.*, hair

crūdelis, -e, *adj.*, cruel

cruentus, -a, -um, *adj.*, bloody

cruor, -ōris, *m.*, blood

cubō, -āre, -uī, -itum, to lie down, recline

cultus, -a, -um, *adj.*, cultivated, refined

cum, *conj.*, when, since, although; *prep.* + *abl.*, with (sometimes suffixed to a pron. as in *mēcum* or *tēcum*)

Cūmānus, -a, -um, *adj.*, Cumaean

cunctus, -a, -um, *adj.*, all

Cupīdō, -inis, *m.*, Cupid, Amor

cupidus, -a, -um, *adj.*, desirous, desiring

cūra, -ae, *f.*, care, anxiety

cūrō (1), to care; to be anxious about

currō, -ere, cucurrī, cursum, to run

currus, -ūs, *m.*, chariot, car

curtus, -a, -um, *adj.*, short, deficient; gelded

curuus, -a, -um, *adj.*, curved

custōdia, -ae, *f.*, watch, guard, guards

custos, -ōdis, *m.*, guard

daps, dapis, *f.*, a sacrificial feast

dē, *prep.* + *abl.*, from, down from; about

decet, -ēre, -uit, to be proper, fitting

dēcidō, -ere, -cidī, -cāsum, to fall down

decus, -oris, *n.*, distinction, grace

dēdicō (1), to dedicate, consecrate

dēdō, -ere, dēdidī, dēditum, to surrender; to dedicate

dēdūcō, -ere, -duxī, -ductum, to bring, lead down; to escort (*sometimes in marriage*)

dēfessus, -a, -um, *adj.*, weary, tired

dēficiō, -ere, -fēcī, -fectum, to fail

dein, deinde, *adv.*, from that place, thereupon, then

dēleō, -ēre, -lēuī, -lētum, to blot out, destroy

Dēlos, -ī, *f.*, Delos, island of Apollo and Diana's birth

Delphicus, -a, -um, *adj.*, related to Delphi

dēmens, -mentis, *adj.*, to be mad, mindless

dēmentia, -ae, *f.*, madness

dens, dentis, *m.*, tooth

densus, -a, -um, *adj.*, close together, dense

dēpellō, -ere, -pulī, -pulsum, to drive away

dēperdō, -ere, -perdidī, -perditum, to lose

dēpōnō, -ere, -posuī, -positum, to put away

dērēpō, -ere, dērepsī, to creep

dēripiō, -ere, -ripuī, -reptum, to snatch away

dēserō, -ere, -seruī, -sertum, to forsake, abandon

dēspiciō, -ere, -spexī, -spectum, to look down; to look down upon

dēspuō, -ere, -spuī, -spūtum, to spit on the ground

dēstituō, -ere, -stituī, -stitūtum, to desert

dēsuescō, -ere, -suēuī, -suētum, to become unaccustomed to

dēterō, -ere, -trīuī, -trītum, to rub away, wear out

dētexō, -ere, -texuī, -textum, to plait or weave

dētineō, -ēre, -tinuī, -tentum, to hold back, detain

dētrahō, -ere, -traxī, -tractum, to draw down; to take away

dēueneror, -ārī, -ātus sum, to worship; to avert by prayers or sacrifice

dēuocō (1), to call down from, summon

dēuoueō, -ēre, -uōuī, -uōtum, to consecrate or devote, *especially to the infernal gods*; to curse

deus, -ī, *m.*, god

dexter, -tra, -trum, *adj.*, right

dīcō, -ere, dixī, dictum, to speak, say

Dictynna, -ae, *f.*, Diana

diēs, -ēī, *m.*, day

difficilis, -e, *adj.*, difficult, obstinate

digitus, -ī, *m.*, finger

dīs, dītis, *adj.*, rich
discēdō, -ere, -cessī, -cessum, to part; to go away
discidium, -ī, *n.*, separation
discō, -ere, didicī, to learn
discors, discordis, *adj.*, disagreeing, opposed
dispōnō, -ere, -posuī, -positum, to distribute, arrange
dīues, -itis, *adj.*, wealthy, rich
dīuitiae, -arum, *f.*, riches
dīuus, -ī, *m.*, god
dō, dare, dedī, dātum, to give
domō, -āre, domuī, domitum, to tame
doceō, -ēre, docuī, doctum, to teach
doleō, -ēre, doluī, dolitum, to be in pain; to grieve
dolor, dolōris, *m.*, pain
dolus, -ī, *m.*, trick, artifice
domina, -ae, *f.*, mistress
dominus, -ī, *m.*, master
domus, -ūs, *f.*, household, house
dōnum, -ī, *n.*, gift
dubitō (1), to hesitate
dubius, -a, -um, *adj.*, unsure
dūcō, -ere, duxī, ductum, to lead
dulcis, -e, *adj.*, sweet
dum, *adv.*, so long as, while; + *subjunctive*, until, provided that
durus, -a, -um, *adj.*, hard
dux, ducis, *m.*, leader

ē, ex, *prep.* + *abl.*, from, away from, out of
ebur, -oris, *n.*, ivory
edō, -ere, ēdī, ēsum, to eat

ēdō, -ere, -didī, -ditum, to put forth
ēducō (1), to raise
ēdūcō, -ere, -duxī, -ductum, to draw out, lead out
efficiō, -ere, -fēcī, -fectum, to do, make
ego, *pron.*, I
ei, *exclamation*, alas, woe
Ēlēus, -a, -um, *adj.*, from Elis
ēliciō, -ere, -licuī, -licitum, to call forth, conjure up
ēlūdō, -ere, -lūsī, -lūsum, to parry a blow, ward off; to deceive
ēmereō, -ēre, -uī, -itum, to obtain by service, to earn pay; to serve out (especially in the military), *hence* to use up, wear out
ēmittō, -ere, -mīsī, -missum, to send out, let loose
ēn, *exclamation*, look!
eō, īre, iī, itum, to go
epulae, -arum, *f.*, dishes, a banquet (often in a religious context)
equa, -ae, *f.*, mare
equus, -ī, *m.*, horse
ēripiō, -ere, -uī, -reptum, to snatch away
errō (1), to wander; to go astray
ērubescō, -ere, -rubuī, to blush
et, *conj.*, and
etiam, *conj.*, still, also, even
ēueniō, -īre, -uēnī, -uentum, to come forth; to turn out
Eurus, -ī, *m.*, the East Wind
excitō (1), to wake, rouse

exclūdō, -ere, -clūsī, -clūsum, to shut, exclude

exerceō, -ēre, -uī, -itum, to work, practice; to make strong

exhibeō, -ēre, -hibuī, -hibitum, to hold out; to produce

exiguus, -a, -um, *adj.*, small, narrow

exitium, -ī, *n.*, destruction

expellō, -ere, -pulī, -pulsum, to drive out

expleō, -ēre, -plēuī, -plētum, to fill

explōrō (1), to investigate, explore

exscreō (1), to cough out

exta, -ōrum, *n. pl.*, entrails of animals

extō (1), to stand out; to be in existence

externus, -a, -um, *adj.*, from the outside, foreign

extruō, -ere, -truxī, -tructum, to heap up, pile up

exuō, -ere, -uī, -ūtum, to lay aside; to strip

exūrō, -ere, -ussī, -ustum, to burn

exuviae, -ārum, *f. pl.*, spoils

fābula, -ae, *f.*, gossip, an idle tale, a fable

faciēs, -ēī, *f.*, appearance, face

facilis, -e, *adj.*, easy, skilled

Falernus, -a, -um, *adj.*, Falernian

fallax, -ācis, *adj.*, deceptive, false

fallō, -ere, fefellī, falsum, to deceive

falx, falcis, *f.*, sickle, pruning hook

fames, -is, *f.*, hunger

fātum, -ī, *n.*, that which is decreed, fate

faueō, -ēre, fāuī, fautum, to favor, support

fauus, -ī, *m.*, honeycomb

fax, facis, *f.*, torch

fel, fellis, *n.*, gall, bile

fēlix, -īcis, *adj.*, happy, fortunate, wealthy

fēmina, -ae, *f.*, woman

fēmineus, -a, -um, *adj.*, feminine, female

ferō, ferre, tulī, lātum, to bear, carry, report; to receive an offering

ferreus, -a, -um, *adj.*, made of iron

ferrūgō, -inis, *f.*, tempered iron, blackish purple

ferrum, -ī, *n.*, iron, a sword

fertilis, -e, *adj.*, fertile

ferus, -a, -um, *adj.*, wild; *as a substantive,* wild beast

fessus, -a, -um, *adj.*, tired, exhausted

fētus, -ūs, *m.*, offspring

fibra, -ae, *f.*, the portion of the liver used in divination

fictilis, -e, *adj.*, earthenware

fides, -eī, *f.*, trust, confidence, fidelity

fīdus, -a, -um, *adj.*, faithful

fīgō, -ere, fixī, fixum, to fix, fasten; to thrust home

fīlum, -ī, *n.*, thread, a woolen fillet

findō, -ere, fidī, fissum, to split

fingō, -ere, finxī, fictum, to
fashion, shape
fīō, fierī, factus sum, to be
made; to become, come into
existence
firmus, -a, -um, *adj.*, firm, strong
fiscella, -ae, *f.*, a small basket
flamma, -ae, *f.*, flame, blaze
flāuus, -a, -um, *adj.*, blonde
fleō, -ēre, -ēuī, -ētum, to weep
flētus, -ūs, *m.*, weeping
flōridus, -a, -um, *adj.*, floral
flōs, flōris, *m.*, flower
flūmen, -inis, *n.*, stream, river
fluō, -ere, fluxī, fluxum, to
flow, drip with
focus, -ī, *m.*, hearth, altar
foedus, -a, -um, *adj.*, foul,
abominable
foedus, -eris, *n.*, contract, pact
fons, fontis, *m.*, spring
foris, -is, *f.*, door
forma, -ae, *f.*, beauty
formōsus, -a, -um, *adj.*,
beautiful, handsome
fors, fortis, *f.*, chance; **Fors**, the
goddess Fortuna
forte, *adv.*, by chance
fortis, -e, *adj.*, strong, brave
fortiter, *adv.*, strongly, bravely
forum, -ī, *n.*, open square, forum
frangō, -ere, frēgī, fractum, to
break, shatter
frēnō (1), to bridle
fretum, -ī, *n.*, strait, channel
frīgus, frīgoris, *n.*, coldness
frons, frondis, *f.*, a leaf, foliage
frons, frontis, *f.*, forehead, brow
fructus, -ūs, *m.*, produce, fruits

fruor, -ī, fructus sum, to have
the benefit of; to enjoy
frustrā, *adv.*, in vain
frux, frūgis, *f.*, fruit of the
earth, a crop
fugiō, -ere, fūgī, fugitum, to flee
fugō (1), to put to flight
fulgō, -ēre, fulsī, to flash; to shine
fulmen, -inis, *n.*, lightning
fuluus, -a, -um, *adj.*, shining
fūmōsus, -a, -um, *adj.*, smoked
fundō, -ere, fūdī, fūsum, to pour
fūnus, -eris, *n.*, funeral
furor, -ōris, *m.*, madness
fūr, fūris, *m.*, thief
furtim, *adv.*, stealthily
furtīuus, -a, -um, *adj.*, stolen,
concealed
furtum, -ī, *n.*, theft
furuus, -a, -um, *adj.*, dark
fuscus, -a, -um, *adj.*, dusky
fūsus, -ī, *m.*, spindle

garrulus, -a, -um, *adj.*, talkative
gaudeō, -ēre, gāuīsus sum, to
rejoice, take pleasure in
gaudium, -ī, *n.*, joy, pleasure
gelidus, -a, -um, *adj.*, frozen
geminō (1), to double
gemma, -ae, *f.*, jewel
gena, -ae, *f.*, cheek
gens, gentis, *f.*, people, nation,
tribe
genu, -ūs, *n.*, knee
gerō, -ere, gessī, gestum, to
carry, bring
gestiō, -īre, to long to (+
infinitive)
glans, glandis, *f.*, acorn

gloria, -ae, *f.*, renown, glory

gracilis, -e, *adj.*, slender

grandis, -e, *adj.*, tall, grown

grātia, -ae, *f.*, pleasantness, favor, thanks

grātus, -a, -um, *adj.*, pleasant, kind, favorable

grauis, -e, *adj.*, heavy, serious

grauiter, *adv.*, gravely, seriously

grex, gregis, *m.*, herd

gypsō (1), to cover with gypsum

habēna, -ae, *f.*, strap; *pl.* reins

habeō, -ēre, habuī, habitum, to have

habilis, -e, *adj.*, useable, at hand

Haemonius, -a, -um, *adj.*, Thessalian

Hecatē, -ae, *f.*, Hecate

herba, -ae, *f.*, herb, grass, green shoot, weed

hesternus, -a, -um, *adj.*, yesterday

heu, *exclamation.*, oh no!

hībernus, -a, -um, *adj.*, winter

hic, haec, hoc, *pron. and adj.*, this

hīc, *adv.*, here

hinc, *adv.*, from here, from this

hircus, -ī, *m.*, he-goat

homō, -inis, *m.*, man

hōra, -ae, *f.*, hour, season

horreō, -ēre, to be rough; to bristle

horridus, -a, -um, *adj.*, rough, shaggy, bristly

hortus, -ī, *m.*, garden

hostia, -ae, *f.*, sacrificial victim

hostilis, -e, *adj.*, enemy

hostis, -is, *m./f.*, enemy

hūc, *adv.*, to here, hither

humus, -ī, *f.*, earth, soil

iaceō, -ēre, -uī, to lie

iactō (1), to throw, cast, fling about

iam, *adv.*, now, at this point

iānitor, -ōris, *m.*, door slave

iānua, -ae, *f.*, door

Idaeus, -a, -um, *adj.*, related to Mt. Ida

īdem, eadem, idem, *pron.*, the same one

ignis, -is, *m.*, fire

ignoscō, -ere, -gnōuī, -gnōtum, to overlook, forgive

ille, illa, illud, *pron. and adj.*, that

illīc, *adv.*, there

imber, imbris, *m.*, rain, storm

imbrifer, -fera, -ferum, *adj.*, rain-bringing

immensus, -a, -um, *adj.*, vast

immītis, -e, *adj.*, pitiless, harsh

imperium, -ī, *n.*, rule, formal authority

imperō (1), to order

impius, -a, -um, *adj.*, sacrilegious, blasphemous

implicō, -ere, -uī, -itum, to enfold, entwine

impōnō, -ere, -posuī, -positum, to place on

imprūdens, -entis, *adj.*, incautious, foolish

impūne, *adv.*, without punishment

in, *prep.* + *acc.*, into; + *abl.*, in, on

incēdō, -ere, -cessī, -cessum, to walk, march, progress

incertus, -a, -um, *adj.,*
uncertain, unsteady
incestus, -a, -um, *adj.,* unfit to
worship, defiled
increpō, -āre, -uī, -itum, to
make a noise, chide
incultus, -a, -um, *adj.,* raw,
uncouth, uncultivated
India, -ae, *f.,* India
indoctus, -a, -um, *adj.,*
unskilled, not learned
indomitus, -a, -um, *adj.,* untamed
ineptus, -a, -um, *adj.,*
inappropriate, foolish
iners -ertis, *adj.,* unskillful,
idle, lazy
inertia, -ae, *f.,* idleness, laziness
inexpertus, -a, -um, *adj.,*
inexperienced, untried
infēlix, -īcis, *adj.,* unhappy,
unfortunate
infernus, -a, -um, *adj.,* from the
underworld
inficiō, -ere, -fēcī, -fectum, to
work in; to dye
infirmus, -a, -um, *adj.,*
unsound, weak
ingerō, -ere, -gessī, -gestum, to
carry in, throw on
inguen, -guinis, *n.,* groin,
private parts
iniustus, -a, -um, *adj.,* unjust,
unfair
innumerus, -a, -um, *adj.,*
countless
inornātus, -a, -um, *adj.,*
unadorned
inriguus, -a, -um, *adj.,*
watering, irrigating; watered

inritus, -a, -um, *adj.,* fruitless,
vain
inserō, -ere, -uī, insertum, to
let in, introduce
insideō, -ēre, insēdī, insessum,
to sit upon
insidiae, -arum, *f. pl.,* ambush
inspērans, -spērantis, *adj.,* not
hoping, not expecting
instabilis, -e, *adj.,* unstable,
inconstant
insuētus, -a, -um, *adj.,*
unaccustomed
interdum, *adv.,* meanwhile
intereā, *adv.,* meanwhile
intereō, -īre, -iī, -itum, to pass
away, die
interpōnō, -ere, -posuī,
-positum, to put between
intonsus, -a, -um, *adj.,* uncut
intortus, -a, -um, *adj.,* twisted
intrā, *adv.,* inside, within
inuītus, -a, -um, *adj.,* unwilling
inultus, -a, -um, *adj.,*
unpunished; unavenged
iō, *exclamation,* ho!
iocōsus, -a, -um, *adj.,* merry
ipse, ipsa, ipsum, *adj. and*
pron., himself, herself, itself
īrātus, -a, -um, *adj.,* angry
is, ea, id, *pron.,* he, she, it
iste, ista, istud, *pron.,* that of
yours
iter, itineris, *n.,* road, way
iubeō, -ēre, iussī, iussum, to
order
iucundus, -a, -um, *adj.,* joyous
iūgerum, -ī, *n.,* a measure of land,
somewhat less than an acre

iugum, -ī, *n.*, yoke, a team of oxen

iuncus, -ī, *m.*, rush

iungō, -ere, iunxī, iunctum, to yoke, join

Iuppiter, Iouis, *m.*, Jupiter

iūrō (1), to swear

ius, iuris, *n.*, law, right

iustus, -a, -um, *adj.*, just, fair

iuuencus, -ī, *m.*, a young bull, bullock

iuuenis, -is, *m.*, youth

iuuentās, -tātis, *f.*, youthfulness

iuuō, -āre, iūuī, iūtum, to help; to delight, please

labor, -ōris, *m.*, struggle, toil

lac, lactis, *n.*, milk

lacertus, -ī, *m.*, arm

lacrima, -ae, *f.*, tear

lacteus, -a, -um, *adj.*, milky

lacus, -ūs, *m.*, vat

laedō, -ere, laesī, laesum, to strike, harm

laetus, -a, -um, *adj.*, glad, happy

languidus, -a, -um, *adj.*, exhausted, spent

lānificus, -a, -um, *adj.*, wool-working

lapis, -idis, *m.*, stone

laqueus, -ī, *m.*, snare, trap

Lār, Laris, *m.*, Lar, household god

lascīuus, -a, -um, *adj.*, playful; licentious; slutty

lassō (1), to exhaust

lateō, -ēre, -uī, to hide

later, -eris, *m.*, a tile; a terracotta weight

Lātōna, -ae, *f.*, Latona

lātus, -a, -um, *adj.*, broad

lātus, -eris, *n.*, flank

laudō (1), to praise

laus, laudis, *f.*, praise

laxus, -a, -um, *adj.*, wide, loose

lectus, -ī, *m.*, bed

lēna, -ae, *f.*, a madam, a procuress

lēnis, -e, *adj.*, gentle

lēniter, *adv.*, gently

lentus, -a, -um, *adj.*, slow, sluggish

leō, -ōnis, *m.*, a lion

leuis, -e, *adj.*, light, fickle, trivial

leuō (1), to lighten, rest

lex, lēgis, *f.*, covenant, law

līber, -bera, -berum, *adj.*, free

libet, -ēre, libuit, libitum, it pleases

lībō (1), to taste

licet, -ēre, licuit, licitum, it is permitted

lignum, -ī, *n.*, log, wood; *pl.*, firewood

līmen, -inis, *n.*, threshold, doorway

līmes, -itis, *m.*, a path, a boundary line

lingua, -ae, *f.*, tongue

linter, -tris, *f.*, a small boat; a tub, a vat

liquidus, -a, -um, *adj.*, flowing

liquor, -ōris, *m.*, liquid, fluid

locus, -ī, *m.*, place, position, occasion

longē, *adv.*, long, at length

longus, -a, -um, *adj.*, long, at length

loquax, -quācis, *adj.*, talkative, speaking

loquor, -ī, locūtus sum, to speak

lūbricus, -a, -um, *adj.*, wet

lūceō, -ēre, luxī, —, to shine

lūcidus, -a, -um, *adj.*, bright

Lūcifer, -ferī, *m.*, the morning star

lucrum, -ī, *n.*, profit, gain

lūdō, -ere, lūsī, lūsum, to play, have fun; to mock

lūmen, -inis, *n.*, light; eye (especially in pl.)

luō, -ere, -ī, -tūrus, to expiate, pay the penalty for (with *poenas*)

lupus, -ī, *m.*, wolf

lustrō (1), to purify

lutum, -ī, *n.*, mud, dirt

luxuria, -ae, *f.*, excess, extravagance

lympha, -ae, *f.*, clear water

madeō, -ēre, to drip; to overflow; to be steeped in

maereō, -ēre, to be sad; to mourn

magicus, -a, -um, *adj.*, magic

magister, -trī, *m.*, director, teacher

magisterium, -ī, *n.*, teaching

magnificus, -a, -um, *adj.*, grandiose, boastful

magnus, -a, -um, *adj.*, great

male, *adv.*, ill, badly

mālō, malle, māluī, to prefer

malus, -a, -um, *adj.*, bad, evil

mānēs, -ium, *m. pl.*, the dead; spirits, ghosts; corpses

manus, -ūs, *f.*, hand

Marathus, -ī, *m.*, Marathus

mare, -is, *n.*, sea

Martius, -a, -um, *adj.*, related to Mars, warlike

mater, matris, *f.*, mother

mātūrō (1), to ripen

mātūrus, -a, -um, *adj.*, ripe, fully grown

Mēdēa, -ae, *f.*, Medea

medicus, -a, -um, *adj.*, medicinal, medical

medius, -a, -um, *adj.*, in the middle of

mel, mellis, *n.*, honey

melius, *adv.*, better, *compar. of* bene

membrum, -ī, *n.*, limb

meminī, -isse, to remember

memorābilis, -e, *adj.*, worthy of remembering, memorable

mensa, -ae, *f.*, table

mens, mentis, *f.*, mind

mereō, -ēre, -uī, -itum, to deserve, earn, merit

merum, -ī, *n.*, undiluted wine

messis, -is, *f.*, harvest

meus, -a, -um, *adj.*, my

migrō (1), to move from one place to another

mīles, -itis, *m.*, soldier

mille, *numeral*, a thousand

mina -ae, *f.*, threat, danger

Minerua, -ae, *f.*, Minerva

minister, -trī, *m.*, ministra, -trae, *f.*, servant, assistant (often to the gods)

ministerium, -ī, *n.*, service, assistance (often in a religious context)

minium, -ī, *n.*, cinnabar, a
  bright red mineral
misceō, -ēre, -uī, mixtum, to
  mix
miser, -era, -erum, wretched,
  unhappy
mītis, -e, *adj.*, mild, sweet
mittō, -ere, mīsī, missum, send
modō (modŏ), *adv.*, only; +
  subjunctive, if only
modulor, -ārī, to measure; to
  play (as an instrument)
modus, -ī, *m.*, manner, mode,
  measure
mola, -ae, *f.*, salted meal (used
  in sacrifices)
mōles, -is, *f.*, a mass, a dam
mollis, -e, *adj.*, soft
mons, montis, *m.*, mountain
mora, -ae, *f.*, delay
morbus, -ī, *n.*, disease
**morior, -ī, mortuus sum,
  moritūrus,** to die
mors, mortis, *f.*, death
mox, *adv.*, soon
mūgītus, -ūs, *m.*, mooing
multus, -a, -um, *adj.*, many, much
mūnus, mūneris, *n.*, duty,
  service, gift
mustum, -ī, *n.*, must, new wine
mūtuus, -a, -um, *adj.*, mutual

nam, *conj.*, for
narrō (1), to recount, tell
nascor, -ī, nātus sum, to be born
-ne, -n, *interrog. enclitic*
nec, *conj.*, and not, nor
nefandus, -a, -um, *adj.*, not to
  be spoken, abominable

neglegō (1), to pay no attention
  to, neglect
negō (1), to deny
Nemesis, -is, *f.*, Nemesis,
  (Tibullus's beloved in
  Book 2, and the goddess of
  vengeance)
nempe, *conj.*, to be sure
Nērēis, -idis, *f.*, a daughter of
  Nereus (a sea god), a Nereid
nesciō (nesciŏ), -īre, -iī, -ītum,
  to not know
neu or **neue** *adv.*, and not, or not
  (especially after *ut* or *ne*)
nexus, -ūs, *m.*, interlacing,
  entwining, knot
nī, nisi, *conj.*, unless, if not
niger, -gra, -grum, *adj.*, black
nihil, *n. indecl.*, nothing
Nīsus, -ī, *m.*, Nisus, king of
  Megara
niteō, -ēre, -uī, -itum, to shine
nitidus, -a, -um, *adj.*, shining,
  aglow
niueus, -a, -um, *adj.*, snowy, pale
nix, niuis, *f.*, snow
noceō, -ēre, -uī, -itum, to harm
nōmen, -inis, *n.*, name
nōn, *particle*, no
noscō, -ere, nōuī, nōtum, to
  become acquainted with; to
  know
noster, nostra, nostrum, *adj.*,
  our, ours
notō (1), to mark, to denote
Notus, -ī, *m.*, South Wind
nouem, *indecl. numeral*, nine
nouerca, -ae, *f.*, stepmother
nouus, -a, -um, *adj.*, new

nox, noctis, *f.*, night; **Nox,** the goddess, night

nūbila, -ōrum, *n. pl.*, clouds

nullus, -a, -um, *adj.*, no, none

num, *interrog. particle introducing a question to which a negative answer is expected*

nūmen, -inis, *n.*, godhead, divine power

numerō (1), to count; to number

nunc, *adv.*, now

nuntius, -a, -um, *adj.*, announcing, bringing news

nūtus, -ūs, *m.*, nod

ō, *interj.*, oh!

oblīuiscor, -ī, oblītus sum, to forget

obrigescō, -ere, -riguī, to become hard, stiff

obscūrus, -a, -um, *adj.*, dark, shadowy

obsequium, -ī, *n.*, compliance, submission

obsideō, -ēre, -sēdī, -sessum, to besiege

obstrepō, -ere, -strepuī, -strepitum, to make a noise; to disturb

obuius, -a, -um, *adj.*, in the way, in front of

occulō, -ere, -uī, -tum, to cover up, hide

occupō (1), to take possession of

occurrō, -ere, -currī, -cursum, to meet up with; to attack

odōrātus, -a, -um, *adj.*, perfumed

olea, -ae, *f.*, olive, the olive tree

omnis, -e, *adj.*, all

opera, -ae, *f.*, exertion, service

operor, -ārī, -ātus sum, to work, be busy; to be engaged in; to be engaged in service (to a deity, in the dat.)

ops, opis, *f.*, abundance, wealth; **Ops,** goddess of abundance

optō (1), to wish

opus, -eris, *n.*, work, labor

orāculum, -ī, *n.*, oracle, prophecy

orbis, -is, *m.*, circle, the sky

orior, -īrī, ortus sum, to spring from; to rise

ōrō (1), to pray

ortus, -ūs, *m.*, rising

ōs, ōris, *n.*, mouth

os, ossis, *n.*, bone

osculum, -ī, *n.*, kiss

ouīle, -is, *n.*, a pen for sheep or goats

ouis, -is, *f.*, sheep

paenitet, -ēre, to cause regret

palam, *adv.*, openly

Palēs, -is, *f.*, Pales

parcō, -ere, pepercī, parsum + *dat.*, to spare, refrain from using

pāreō, -ēre, to obey

parō (1), to prepare

paruus, -a, -um, *adj.*, small

pascō, -ere, pāuī, pastum, to pasture, feed; to use as pasturage

passim, *adv.*, everywhere

pastor, -ōris, *m.*, shepherd

pateō, -ēre, -uī, -itum, to stand open, to be open

pater, patris, *m.,* father

patescō, -ere, patuī, to be opened, to become open

patior, -ī, passus sum, to suffer

patrius, -a, -um, *adj.,* paternal, ancestral, native

paulātim, *adv.,* little by little

pauper, -peris, *adj.,* not wealthy, poor

peccō (1), to do wrong

pectō, -ere, pexī, pexum, to comb

pectus, -oris, *n.,* chest

pecus, -oris, *n.,* herd, cattle

pecus, -udis, *f.,* animal

Pēleus, -eos, *m.,* Peleus, king of Thessaly, father of Achilles

pellō, -ere, pepulī, pulsum, to strike; to set in motion, *especially in music*

Pelops, -opis, *m.,* Pelops, son of Tantalus, father of Atreus and Thyestes

pendeō, -ēre, pependī, to hang suspended

pendō, -ere, pependī, pensum, to cause to hang; to weigh

pensum, -ī, *n.,* a portion of wool weighed out for a spinner

per, *prep.* + *acc.,* through, by

peragō, -ere, perēgī, peractum, to do, accomplish

percutiō, -ere, -cussī, -cussum, to strike

perdiscō, -ere, -didicī, to learn thoroughly

perdomō, -āre, -domuī, -domitum, to tame thoroughly

peredō, -esse, -ēdī, -ēsum, to eat through

pereō, -ēre, perī, peritum, to die

periūrium, -ī, *n.,* false swearing, perjury

permittō, -ere, -mīsī, -missum, to let go; to allow

perrēpō, -ere, -repsī, -repsum, to creep over

persoluō, -ere, -uī, -solūtum, to unloose; to pay, pay off; to fulfill

perstō, -stāre, -stitī, -stātum, to stand firm, persist

persuādeō, -ēre, -suāsī, -suāsum, to persuade, to convince

pēs, pedis, *m.,* foot; metrical foot

petō, -ere, -īuī, petītum, to seek; to attack

Phoebus, -ī, *m.,* Phoebus Apollo

Phrygius, -a, -um, *adj.,* Phrygian, from Phrygia in Asia Minor

Pīeris, -idis, *f.,* Muse

piger, -gra, -um, *adj.,* sluggish, numbing

piget, -ere, -uit, -itum, to cause disgust or annoyance

pingō, -ere, pinxī, pictum, to paint, decorate, adorn

pinguis, -e, *adj.,* fat, rich

piscis, -is, *m.,* fish

placeō, -ēre, placuī, placitum, to please

placidus, -a, -um, *adj.,* calming, peaceful, well disposed < *placeō* plānus, -a, -um, *adj.*, flat

plaustrum, -ī, *n.*, wagon

plēnus, -a, -um, *adj.*, full

plūma, -ae, *f.*, feather

plūrimus, -a, -um, *adj.*, very many, most; *superl. of* multus

plūs, plūris, *adj.*, many, more; *compar. of* multus

pluuia, -ae, *f.*, rain

pōculum, -ī, *n.*, drinking cup

podagra, -ae, *f.*, gout

poena, -ae, *f.*, penalty; Poena, the goddess of punishment

poēta, -ae, *m.*, poet

pollex, -icis, *m.*, thumb

polliceor, -ērī, pollicitus sum, to promise

polluō, -ere, -uī, -ūtum, to defile, pollute

pōmōsus, -a, -um, *adj.*, fruit laden

pōmum, -ī, *n.*, fruit

pōmus, -ī, *f.*, fruit tree

pondus, -eris, *n.*, weight

pōnō, -ere, posuī, positum, to put, place, put to one side

pontus, -ī, *m.*, sea

pōpulus, -ī, *f.*, poplar tree

portō (1), carry

possum, posse, potuī, to be able

post, *adv.*, after, behind; *prep.* + *acc.*, after, behind

postis, -is, *m.*, door-post

potior, -us, *adj.*, preferable, better than

praebeō, -ēre, -buī, -bitum, to offer

praeceptum, -ī, *n.*, lesson

praecinō, -ere, -cinuī, -centum, to sing before

praecordia, -ōrum, *n. pl.*, chest, the heart

praeda, -ae, *f.*, loot, plunder

praedātor, -ōris, *m.*, looter, plunderer

praeferō, -ferre, -tulī, -lātum, to bear before, display

praemium, -ī, *n.*, prize, reward

praesepium, -ī, *n.*, manger, stall

praestō, *adv.*, at hand

praetemptō (1), to try beforehand

praetereō, -īre, -iī, -itum, to go past

praetexō, -ere, -uī, -textum, to weave before; to fringe

precor, -ārī, -ātus sum, to pray, entreat

premō, -ere, pressī, pressum, to press, oppress

pretium, -ī, *n.*, price, reward

prex, precis, *f.*, entreaty, prayer

Priapus, -ī, *m.*, Priapus

prīmō, *adv.*, at first

prīmum, *adv.*, at first

prīmus, -a, -um, *adj.*, first

prior, prius, *adj.*, former, first, prior

priscus, -a, -um, *adj.*, first, ancient

prius, *adv.*, before

prō, *prep.* + *abl.*, on behalf of whom, for

procul, *adv.*, far, far away

prōcumbō, -ere, -cubuī, -cubitum, to bend forward; to lie prostrate

prōcūrō (1), to take care

prōdeō, -īre, -iī, -itum, to go forth, advance

prōdūcō, -ere, -duxī, -ductum, to extend, draw out, endure

prōferō, -ferre, -tulī, -lātum, to bring forth

prōles, -is, *f.*, offspring

prope, *adv.*, near

propior, -us, *adj.*, nearer, closer

prōspiciō, -ere, -spexī, -spectum, to look forward, look out

prōsum, prōdesse, prōfuī, to benefit, profit

prōuocō (1), to call forth

pūbēs, -is, *f.*, youth

pudeō, -ēre, puduī, to be ashamed; *often impers.*, it causes shame (with gen. of cause)

pudor, -ōris, *m.*, shame, modesty

puella, -ae, *f.*, girl

puer, -ī, *m.*, boy

pugnō (1), to fight

pullus, -a, -um, *adj.*, dark, gloomy

puluis, -eris, *m.*, dust, sand

pūniceus, -a, -um, *adj.*, purple, red

puppis, -is, *f.*, the stern, a ship

purgō (1), to clean, cleanse

purpureus, -a, -um, *adj.*, purple-colored, dark violet

purus, -a, -um, *adj.*, pure, clean, unadorned; purifying

pussula, -ae, *f.*, blister, pustule

putō (1), to consider

Pȳthō, -ūs, *f.*, Pytho (the old name for Delphi)

quaerō *or* **quaesō, -ere, quaesīuī, quaestum**, to seek

quālibet, *adv.*, anywhere

quam, *adv.*, how; than; as

quamuīs, *conj.*, although

quantum, *n.*, how much?

queō, -īre, quiī, quitum, to be able

querella, -ae, *f.*, complaint

quernus, -a, -um, *adj.*, oaken

queror, -ī, questus sum, to complain, lament

quia, *adv.*, because

quī, quae, quod, *rel. pron.*, who, what, which; *adj.*, any

quīcumque, quaecumque, quodcumque, *pron.*, whoever, whatever

quīdam, quaedam, quoddam, *pron.*, a certain person or thing, someone, something

quīn, *conj.*, rather, but

quis, quid, *pron.*, *adj.* who, what; why (neuter only)

quisquam, quaequam, quidquam, *pron.*, anyone, anything

quisque, quaeque, quidque, *pron.*, each, every, everyone

quisquis, quaequae, quidquid, *pron.*, whoever, whichever, whatever; anyone, anything, any

quod, *conj.*, because; the fact that

quondam, *adv.*, once

quoque, *adv.*, also

quotannīs, *adv.*, every year

quotiens, *adv.*, how many times

rapax, -ācis, *adj.*, greedy
rapidus, -a, -um, *adj.*, grasping, swift
rapiō, -ere, -uī, raptum, to seize, take
ratis, -is, *f.*, raft, boat
recubō (1), to recline
recurrō, -ere, -ī, -cursum, to run back
reddō, -ere, -didī, -ditum, to give back, restore, give as due
redeō, -īre, -iī, -itum, come back, return
referō, -ferre, -ttulī, -latum, to take back, return, repeat, recall
refugiō, -ere, -fūgī, to run away
regnum, -ī, *n.*, royal power, a kingdom
relinquō, -ere, -līquī, -lictum, to leave behind, abandon
remeō (1), to return
rēmus, -ī, *m.*, oar
renuō, -ere, -nuī, to nod back in disapproval; to refuse
requiescō, -ere, -quiēuī, -quiētum, to rest
requīrō, -ere, -quīsiī, -quīsītum, to ask, look for
rēs, reī, *f.*, thing, matter, wealth
reserō (1), to unlock, unbolt
resoluō, -ere, -soluī, -solūtum, to unbind, release, free
respondeō, -ēre, -spondī, -sponsum, to answer
rēte, -is, *n.*, net
retineō, -ēre, -uī, retentum, to hold, retain

rīdeō, -ēre, rīsī, rīsum, to laugh, laugh at
rītus, -ūs, *m.*, ceremony, rite
rīuus, -ī, *m.*, stream bank, shore
rixa, -ae, *f.*, brawl, tussle
rōbur, -oris, *n.*, hard wood, strength
rogō (1), to ask
rogus, -ī, *m.*, funeral pyre
rostrum, -ī, *n.*, beak, the curved end of the prow of a ship
rota, -ae, *f.*, wheel
rubeō, -ēre, to be red
ruber, -bra, -brum, *adj.*, red
rubor, -ōris, *m.*, redness, a blush, shame
rumpō, -ere, rūpī, ruptum, break, rupture
rūs, rūris, *n.*, the country
rusticus, -a, -um, *adj.*, rural, country, uncouth, boorish,

sacer, sacra, sacrum, *adj.*, sacred
sacrō (1), dedicate, consecrate
sacculum, ī, *n.*, age, era
saepe, *adv.*, often
saeuiō, -īre, -iī, -ītum, to rage, be fierce, be cruel to
saeuus, -a, -um, *adj.*, cruel, savage, fierce
sāga, -ae, *f.*, wise woman, witch
sagitta, -ae, *f.*, arrow
salūbris, -e, *adj.*, healthful
saluus, -a, -um, *adj.*, healthy, safe
Samius, -a, -um, *adj.*, Samian, from the island of Samos
sanctus, -a, -um, *adj.*, holy, sacred
sanguineus, -a, -um, *adj.*, bloody

sanguis, -inis, *m.*, blood
sānō (1), to make healthy, cure
satiō (1), to satisfy; to overfill
satiō, -ōnis, *f.*, sowing
satur, -tura, -turum, *adj.*, sated, full, rich
saxum, -ī, *n.*, stone
sciō, -īre, -iī, -ītum, to know
sē, *refl. pron.*, himself, herself, itself
secō, -āre, secuī, sectum, to cut
sector, -ārī, -ātus sum, to follow after
secundus, -a, -um, *adj.*, following, favorable
sēcurus, -a, -um, *adj.*, without a care, secure; *poetic*, to make carefree
sed, *conj.*, but
sēdēs, -is, *m.*, seat, home
sēdulus, -a, -um, *adj.*, attentive, diligent
seges, -etis, *f.*, a field planted with mature grain
segnis, -e, *adj.*, sluggish
sēligō, -ere, -lēgī, -lectum, to choose, pick out
semel, *adv.*, once
sēmen, sēminis, *n.*, seed
semper, *adv.*, ever, always
senecta, -ae, *f.*, old age
senex, senis, *m.*, old man
sentiō, -īre, sensī, sensum, to feel, sense
sepulcrum, -ī, *n.*, tomb
sequor, -ī, secūtus sum, to follow
sera, -ae, *f.*, bolt, lock
serēnus, -a, -um, *adj.*, bright, fair
serō, -ere, sēuī, satum, to sow

serpens, -entis, *m.*, snake
sertum, -ī, *n.*, wreath, garland
seruiō, -īre, to be subject to; to be a slave
seruitium, -ī, *n.*, service, slavery
serum, -ī, *n.*, whey
seruō (1), to watch over
sērus, -a, -um, *adj.*, late
seruus, -ī, *m.*, slave
seu *or* **sīue**, *conj.*, or if; **seu (sīue) . . . seu (sīue)**, whether . . . or
sī, *conj.*, if
sīc, *adv.*, thus, in this way
siccus, -a, -um, *adj.*, dry
sīdus, -eris, *n.*, star
significō (1), to give a sign
signum, -ī, *n.*, sign, military standard
sileō, -ēre, -uī, to be still, noiseless
silex, silicis, *m.*, flint
simulō (1), to imitate, to seem
sine, *prep. + abl.*, without
singulus, -a, -um, *adj.*, single, each
sinō, -ere, sīuī, situm, to allow, permit
sinus, -ūs, *m.*, bend, curve, lap, breast; *often* the fold of the toga (used as a pocket)
sitis, -is, *f.*, thirst
smaragdus, -ī, *m.*, an emerald or other precious stone
sōbrius, -a, -um, *adj.*, sober; *poetic,* making *or* keeping sober
sōl, sōlis, *m.*, sun
soleō, -ēre, -uī, -itum, to accustom
sollertia, -ae, *f.*, cleverness, skill

solum, -ī, *n.*, soil
soluō, -ere, soluī, solūtum, to loosen; to release from
sōlus, -a, -um, *adj.*, alone, only
somnium, -ī, *n.*, dream
somnus, -ī, *m.*, sleep
sonitus, -ūs, *m.*, sound, noise
sonō, -āre, sonuī, sonitum, to make a noise
sonus, -ī, *m.*, sound
sopor, -ōris, *m.* deep sleep
soror, -ōris, *f.* sister
spargō, -ere, sparsī, sparsum, sprinkle
spectō (1), to look at, contemplate
spernō, -ere, sprēuī, sprētum, to reject, despise
spēs, -eī, *f.*, hope, expectation
spīca, -ae, *f.*, an ear of grain
spīceus, -a, -um, *adj.*, made of ears of grain
stabulum, -ī, *n.*, stall
stella, -ae, *f.*, star
sterilis, -e, *adj.*, sterile
stimulō (1), to goad
stimulus, -ī, *m.*, goad
stīpes, -itis, *m.*, stump, post
stō, stāre, stētī, statum, to stand
strāgulum, -ī, *n.*, spread, covering
strepitus, -ūs, *m.* clattering
strīdor, -ōris, *m.*, screeching, shrieking
strix, strigis, *f.*, a screech owl
stultē, *adv.*, stupidly, foolishly
stultus, -a, -um, *adj.*, stupid, foolish
sub, *prep.* + *abl.*, underneath; *prep.* + *acc.*, along under, up under

subdō, -ere, -didī, -ditum, to place under
subeō, -īre, -iī, -itum, to pass under; to undergo
subiciō, -ere, -iēcī, -iectum, to throw, place under; to throw up from below, raise
subigō, -ere, -ēgī, -actum, to turn under
subrēpō, -ere, -repsī, to creep up
subsum, -esse, ——, to be under
suffundō, -ere, -fūdī, -fūsum, to pour over
sulcō (1), to plough
sulcus, -ī, *m.*, furrow
sulpur, -uris, *n.*, sulphur
sum, esse, fuī, futūrus, to be
sumō, -ere, sumpsī, sumptum, to take up.
superbus, -a, -um, *adj.*, proud
superō (1), to surpass, overcome
superus, -a, -um, *adj.*, above, upper
supplex, -icis, *adj.*, kneeling, suppliant
suppōnō, -ere, -posuī, -positum, to put under
surgō, -ere, surrexī, surrectum, to rise, get up
suspendō, -ere, -pendī, -pensum, to hang up

taciturnus, -a, -um, *adj.*, silent
tacitus, -a, -um, *adj.*, mute, silent
taeda, -ae, *f.*, a pine torch
taedium, -ī, *n.*, weariness, boredom
tālis, -e, *adj.*, of such a kind, such

tamen, *conj.*, nonetheless, however

tantus, -a, -um, *adj.*, so great

tardō (1), to slow

tardus, -a, -um, *adj.*, slow

taurus, -ī, *m.*, bull

tectum, -ī, *n.*, roof

tegō, -ere, texī, tectum, to cover

tēla, -ae, *f.*, loom

tellus, -ūris, *f.*, earth

templum, -ī, *n.*, temple

temptō (1), to try, make a trial of

tempus, -oris, *n.*, a division, time; *in pl.* temples of the head

tenebrae, -ārum, *f. pl.*, darkness, night

teneō, -ēre, -uī, -tum, to hold, possess, control

tener, -era, -erum, *adj.*, tender

tenuis, -e, *adj.*, thin, fine

tepidus, -a, -um, *adj.*, warm

ter, *adv.*, three times

tercentēnī, -ae, -a, *adj.*, three hundred

tergeō, -ere, tersī, tersum, to wipe, dry off

tergum, -ī, *n.*, back

terō, -ere, trīuī, trītum, to rub, wear away; to thresh

terra, -ae, *f.*, earth, clay, land

terreō, -ēre, -uī, -itum, to frighten

testa, -ae, *f.*, wine jug

texō, -ere, -uī, textum, to weave

textrix, -trīcis, *f.*, weaver

Thetis, -idos, *f.*, Thetis, mother of Achilles

tibia, -ae, *f.*, pipe, flute

tigillum, -ī, *n.*, a small beam

timeō, -ēre, -uī, to fear

timidē, *adv.*, fearfully

timor, -ōris, *m.*, fear

Titius, -ī, *m.*, Titius

toga, -ae, *f.*, toga

torqueō, -ēre, torsī, tortum, to twist, torture

torreō, -ēre, -uī, tostum, to bake, burn

tōrus, -ī, *m.*, couch, bed, marriage bed

tōtus, -a, -um, *adj.*, entire, whole

tractō (1), to haul; to manage; to traffic in

trādō, -ere, -didī, -ditum, to hand over, pass down

trādūcō, -ere, -duxī, -ductum, to carry over, transfer

trahō, -ere, traxī, tractum, to draw, drag, prolong

transeō, -īre, -iī, -itum, to go through, pass, pass by

transgredior, -ī, -gressus sum, to step across, pass over

tremulus, -a, -um, *adj.*, trembling, shaky

trepidus, -a, -um, *adj.*, fearful, causing fear

tristis, -e, *adj.* sad, harsh

Triuia, -ae, *f.*, the goddess of the crossroads, Hecate, Diana

triuium, -ī, *n.*, crossroads

triumphus, -ī, *m.*, a triumphal procession

trux, trūcis, *adj.*, savage, fierce

tū, *pron.* you (sing.)

tuba, -ae, *f.*, war trumpet

tum, *adv.*, then

tumultus, -ūs, *m.*, uproar, hubbub

tunc, *adv.*, then

tundō, -ere, tutudī, tūsum, to beat, pound

tunica, -ae, *f.*, tunic

turba, -ae, *f.*, crowd

turben, -inis, *m.*, a top

turpis, -e, *adj.*, ugly, shameful

tūtus, -a, -um, *adj.*, safe, protected

Tyrius, -a, -um, *adj.*, Tyrian, dyed purple in the fashion of Tyre

Tyros, -ī, *f.*, Tyre

uacca, -ae, *f.*, cow

uagor, -ārī, -ātus sum, to wander

uagus, -a, -um, *adj.*, wandering, restless

ualeō, -ēre, to be healthy, strong, *used in the imperative or subjunctive as a word of farewell or greeting*

ualidus, -a, -um, *adj.*, strong, competent

ualle, -is, *f.*, a valley

uānus, -a, -um, *adj.*, empty

uarius, -a, -um, *adj.*, assorted, varied, various

ubi (ubī), *adv.*, where, when

uehō, -ere, uexī, uectum, to carry, convey

uel, *conj.*, or

uellus, -eris, *n.*, wool, fleece

uelō (1), to cover, veil

uēlox, -ōcis, *adj.*, quick, rapid

uendō, -ere, -didī, -ditum, to sell

ueneror, -ārī, to worship

ueniō, -īre, uēnī, uentum, to come

uentus, -ī, *m.*, wind

Venus, Veneris, *f.*, Venus, goddess of love; *as a common noun*, love

uērax, -ācis, *adj.*, truthful

uerber, -is, *n.*, whip, lash, blow

uerberō (1), to beat, flog

uerbum, -ī, *n.*, word

uerna, -ae, *m./f.*, a house-born slave

uernus, -a, -um, *adj.*, spring

uersō (1), to turn often, to handle

uertō, -ere, uertī, uersum, to turn

uestīgium, -ī, *n.*, track, trace

uestis, -is, *f.*, clothes, garment

uetō, -āre, uetuī, uetitum, to forbid

uetus, ueteris, *adj.*, old, ancient

uia, -ae, *f.*, passage, road; stripe

uīcīnus, -a, -um, *adj.*, neighboring, nearby

uicis, -is, *f.*, change, interchange, alternation

uictus, -ūs, *m.*, manner or life, nourishment

uideō, -ēre, uīdī, uīsum, to see

uigilō (1), to be awake; to keep awake

uīlis, -e, *adj.*, cheap, worthless

uilla, -ae, *f.*, rural estate

uillōsus, -a, -um, *adj.*, shaggy, hairy

uīmen, -inis, *n.*, a twig, shoot, or osier

uinciō, -īre, uinxī, uinctum,
to bind

uinclum, -ī, *n.,* chain, bond

uincō, -ere, uīcī, uictum, to
conquer, overcome

uīnum, -ī, *n.,* wine

uiolentus, -a, -um, *adj.,* violent,
furious

uiolō (1), to offend, do violence to

uir, uirī, *m.,* man, husband

uirga, -ae, *f.,* green twig, a rod,
branch

uirgineus, -a, -um, *adj.,*
maidenly, innocent

uirgō, -inis, *f.,* maiden, an
unmarried woman

uiridis, -e, *adj.,* green

uīta, -ae, *f.,* life

uītis, -is, *f.,* vine

uitium, -ī, *n.,* fault, defect

uītō (1), to avoid

uitulus, -ī, *m./f.,* calf

uīuō, -ere, uixī, uictum, to live

ullus, -a, -um, *adj.,* any

ululō (1), to shriek

umbra, -ae, *f.,* shadow, shade

umbrōsus, -a, -um, *adj.,* shady

umeō, -ēre, to be wet, moist

umerus, -ī, *m.,* shoulder

unda, -ae, *f.,* wave

ūnus, -a, -um, *adj.,* one, alone

uocō (1), call

uolitō (1), to fly about

uolō, uelle, uoluī, to want, wish

uōmer, -meris, *m.,* ploughshare

uōs, *pron.,* you (pl.)

uōtum, -ī, *n.,* promise, vow,
wishes

uox, uōcis, *f.,* voice

urbs, urbis, *f.,* city, *often* Rome

urgeō, -ēre, ursī, to push, press,
drive

urō, -ere, ussī, ustum, to burn;
to brand

usque, *adv.,* continually, forever

usus, -ūs, *m.,* use, making use of

ut, *conj. + indicative,* as, when;
conj. + subjunctive, so that,
with the result that

uterque, utraque, utrumque,
adj., each of two, both

ūtor, -ī, ūsus sum, to use

uua, -ae, *f.,* grape

Vulcānus, -ī, *m.,* Vulcan, god of
the forge and fire

uulnerō (1), to wound

uulnus, -eris, *n.,* wound

uxor, -ōris, *f.,* wife